Battleground

SOMME

Thiepval

With the continued expansion of the Battleground series a **Battleground Europe Club** has been formed to benefit the reader. The purpose of the Club is to keep members informed of new titles and key developments by way of a quarterly newsletter, and to offer many other reader-benefits. Membership is free and by registering an interest you can help us predict print runs and thus maintain prices at their present levels. Please call the office 01226 734555, or send your name and address along with a request for more information to:
Battleground Europe Club Pen & Sword Books Ltd, 47 Church Street, Barnsley, South Yorkshire S70 2AS

Cover illustration by courtesy of Belfast City Council

Battleground Europe

SOMME
Thiepval

Michael Stedman

Series editor
Nigel Cave

LEO COOPER
London

First published in 1995
Reprinted 1997, 2000 by
LEO COOPER
an imprint of
Pen & Sword Books Limited
47 Church Street, Barnsley, South Yorkshire S70 2AS

ISBN 0 85052 473 3

A CIP catalogue of this book is available
from the British Library

Printed by Redwood Books Limited
Trowbridge, Wiltshire

For up-to-date information on other titles produced under the Leo Cooper imprint,
please telephone or write to:

Pen & Sword Books Ltd, FREEPOST, 47 Church Street
Barnsley, South Yorkshire S70 2AS
Telephone 01226 734222

Opposite: Thiepval Chateau's ruins, on the horizon, photographed during the summer of 1916 from British positions in Thiepval Wood.

CONTENTS

ACKNOWLEDGMENTS

Much of what is said within these pages is the product of words penned in haste amidst terrible danger more than eighty years ago. To the diarists, adjutants and ordinary soldiers who wrote at that time and the memoir writers of the post war era I am grateful and can only stand in awe. However, it would have been impossible to complete this guide without the help of many of my contemporaries. In particular I should like to thank Martine Ahamed, David Atherton, Nigel Cave who has undertaken a thorough review of this work and for whose sensible guidance and help I am very grateful; John Garwood, Gerry Gee and Derek Butler and other staff of the Commonwealth War Graves Commission at Maidenhead, Peter Hart, David Kelsall who generously produced some of the illustrations, Tom May, Klaus Spath, Mike Nicholson, Katie Doar and Phil Nash of Waterstones' Booksellers whose excellent specialized maps department, at 17 St. Ann's Square, Manchester, supplied my maps and through whom the requisite present day IGN maps of France can be obtained; Peter Taylor whose library of photographic sources has been invaluable to me, Geoff Thomas, Ralph Whitehead who has provided me with a wealth of photographs, detailed information and translations of German documents, Crispin Worthington, Major George Stephens MBE of the Regimental Museum of the Royal Inniskilling Fusiliers. Major J.N. McConnell of the Royal Irish Fusiliers Regimental Museum. Stuart Eastwood of the Regimental Museum of the Border Regiment and the Kings Own Royal Border Regiment. David Campbell of the Somme Association Ltd. Tony Sprason of the Lancashire Fusiliers Museum in Bury. Dennis Waring and Belfast City Council. The staff at the Public Records Office in Kew have provided me with much help, assistance and considered judgement. Many members of the Western Front Association have also helped in greatly enhancing my knowledge of the Thiepval area. To all of these people I should like to extend my sincere thanks whilst making clear that any errors which remain within the text are solely of my own making. I am also grateful to the Crowood Press for their kind permission to quote from *A Sergeant-Major's War* by Ernest Shephard.

SENSIBLE EQUIPMENT AND ADVICE FOR VISITORS

One of the greatest pleasures, and the most salutary and moving of experiences, is to 'walk the course' of an event in the extraordinary history of the Great War, reconstructing in our minds the encounters of the men who were there and sharing the chance insights and discoveries with friends. For me, like so many other people, the first course was that fatal and tragic route taken by the Newfoundlanders. Later came the Salford Pals, here below Thiepval. But whoever you are following, or whatever you are trying to explain and understand, certain items are always likely to enhance your pleasure. Stout shoes or walking boots at any time of the year. Wellington boots and thick socks in winter or soon after rain. Appropriate outer clothing. A compass. A present day map, of which the most useful are the IGN Blue Series maps to a scale of 1:25,000 entitled Bapaume East and Bapaume West (2407 est et ouest).[1] A trench map (see note under List of Maps). The IGN Green Series 1:100,000 will also help you find and navigate the area by car. For those enthusiasts spending longer in the field and who want to record your visit carefully some further items are advisable. A camera. A pen and notebook to record where you took your photographs and perhaps to note your visit in the cemetery registers. A drink, a sandwich, a decent penknife with a corkscrew, a first aid kit and a shoulder bag for everything.

Here in Thiepval a metal detector is, let us be frank, an embarrassment. To be seen digging within sight of what should be a place of pilgrimage is almost to desecrate the memory of those whose names are recorded so starkly here. The spectacle of lone Britons sweeping their electronic plates across empty fields fills me with sadness. This is a place where a more rewarding and significant history reveals itself, without recourse to indignity.

No significant preparation is required to cope with medical requirements. It is however very sensible to ensure that you carry an E111 form which gives reciprocal rights to medical and hospital treatment in France, as well as all other EC countries. The necessary documents can be obtained free from any main post office. As in the UK where you are in a working agricultural area and may be scratched or cut by rusty metals, ensure that your tetanus vaccination is up to date. Comprehensive personal and vehicle insurance is advisable, at the very least Green Card insurance (often available free from your vehicle insurers) is a legal requirement when motoring abroad. In this context it is worth noting that there have been an increasing number of thefts from

British tourist's vehicles in the area of the Somme, even when parked near to the many well frequented and busy memorials around Thiepval. To help arrange and plan your stay I have identified a list of campsites, hotels and B&B accommodation within easy distance of Thiepval in Chapter 1, which deals with the designated area today. However, a fuller guide to the many excellent hotels, restaurants, auberges and overnight accommodations available in the Picardie area can be obtained from the Comite Regional du Tourisme de Picardie, 3 Rue Vincent Auriol – 80000 Amiens – Tel: 00 33 322 91 10 15.

Le Triomphateur **There are no German military cemeteries in the vicinity of Thiepval, and only one relatively small French military cemetery which shares the space in front of the Memorial to the Missing at Thiepval. In view of the vast numbers of casualties suffered by these two combatants around Thiepval and the nearby ridge between the autumns of 1914 and 1915 this is initially surprising. In fact many of the German dead were taken to the quarries at Miraumont where their remains were destroyed during the period of enormous distrust between the peoples of France and Germany during the post war era. The remains of the French soldiers killed here were concentrated in the French National Cemetery near Albert.**

INTRODUCTION

The experience of war at Thiepval moved many men to write with an authority and power which the passage of time has not in any way diminished. Anticipating the distant future whilst writing in 1929 Charles Douie, who fought at Thiepval, wrote that, "For many years to come stray travellers will revisit the ground where once they fought and endured, where many of their friends lie for ever. But the time must come when the travellers are seen no more, and only the forest of graves above the Ancre will remain to tell the tale of that island race whose sons once were lords of these woods and fields." Today the different interpretations which people, who often have no experience of conflict, place on such words can mean that Douie's understanding of the war can seem out of place in a Europe changed far beyond those distant soldier's imaginings. However, it would be an ill advised person who sought to avoid the many and varied lessons of history. Those who claim that "the path to the future is not through the past" often come to regret such words. By the same token there is of course no golden age to which we can or should return, but to shun consideration of the bleakest or best episodes in man's experience will only breed falsity and weaken the foundations of the future.

In this context Thiepval is one of life's finest classrooms and it is possible to see many visiting groups and individuals sampling the extraordinary history here. A common failing of many such visits is a tendency to 'do' too much. First stop Serre, then Newfoundland Park and onto Thiepval for lunch, followed by la Boisselle, Pozieres and the Butte de Warlencourt before returning to the hotel in Arras, exhausted and perhaps little the wiser! And tomorrow will be Ypres. Yet such places are powerful, evocative and emotionally exhausting, especially for the young upon whom they can make a great impression. To skimp them is like 'doing' Westminster Abbey in five minutes. To trivialize by rushing will simply undermine what could be learned. You cannot marvel at, learn from and treasure the new understanding of something when you are exhausted, and the Somme battlefield is no exception. Much better to halve your itinerary and manage the time you can have here sensibly. Get to know this magnificent location of Thiepval in depth. Let careful observation and thoughtful questioning reveal all of the many layers of fact, insight and interpretation to yourself, your school party or your family and friends.

The village of Thiepval is like no other place with which I am familiar. Although at once a working community, the centrepiece of a past and tragic military enterprise and the location of many memorials, it does not possess the easy repose and tranquillity of some other places of great historical significance. In winter its exposed slopes are a home to a determined and bitter wind which chills the stone and brickwork of the immense Memorial to the Missing. In spring, summer and autumn it is an almost automatic stop for many dozens of coach-parties, pilgrims and the curious. In many of these visitor's eyes the memorial is at once both ugly and enormously moving. From its vantage point you can see more of the Somme and Ancre Battlefields than from virtually any other location. It is no wonder then that during 1915-16 and 1918 it became the centre of a dogged and fiercely contested battle for the supremacy and observation which this ridge conferred on whoever held the village and the nearby Schwaben Redoubt.

The choice of Thiepval as the location for the Memorial to the Missing almost invariably means that it is very often spoken of in terms of the disaster which befell the British Army at the start of their 'Great Push' on the morning of 1st July, 1916. Nearly 20,000 were killed before breakfast had been eaten in London. Within five months the bodies of some 70,000 souls released from the torture of war had been lost without trace, often sunk in the quagmire, sometimes terribly blown apart or simply unrecognizable because of the decay and loss of documents and identity tags if they were found. In perpetuity the names of those men whose bodies were simply unidentifiable or were never found are recorded on the great stone slabs of the enormous structure which dominates the village and its surrounding area.[2]

Thiepval is therefore more frequently visited than almost any other location along the fearful line which became known as 'The Western Front'. But Thiepval is much more than a clinically fortified village in front of which hundreds of men from Salford, Newcastle, Belfast and elsewhere fell on 1st July 1916. Its dominant influence spread far across the Somme Battlefield. Throughout the entirety of 1916 it was contested and coveted by the opposing armies from Britain, her Empire and Germany. Yet before the outbreak of war Thiepval had been a small community, sixty homes, a few of which were farms with suitable outbuildings and stores, a church and the imposing chateau owned by the de Bredas family. On arrival in Thiepval today the first time visitor will be moved by what can be easily seen within half a mile of the great memorial. And it is often best seen some distance from the many visitors who can make quiet reflection difficult. Try looking across

val
ge
Albert
Authuille in
Ancre Valley
Thiepval
Wood

Scene of the Salford Pals' assault on Thiepval, viewed from the area between Mill Road Cemetery and Schwaben Redoubt, looking towards Authuille Village and Albert.

to Thiepval from Connaught Cemetery along the Thiepval Road, then you can begin to see the panorama of the battlefield and understand why so many thousands of Ulstermen and Pals lost their lives here. A family visiting the nearby cemeteries or the memorial, perhaps to recall the life and loss of a relative, now distant in time, will certainly be both proud and also aware of the fragile hold we have on life. But for the serious 'student' of the Great War this is an area which will repay care and study a thousand times over. To all of you I hope that this guide will prove an invaluable aid to your visit. To everyone who sees it, the vastness of the memorial stands as a certain reminder of the folly of war. In such a location there can be no such person as a 'casual visitor'.

The scope covered by this guide touches on the villages of Bouzincourt, Martinsart and Mesnil to the rear of the British lines. Closer to the British front lines lay the villages of Aveluy and Authuille. Astride the River Ancre and within the British positions facing Thiepval lay three vital woodlands, Aveluy, Authuille and Thiepval Woods. In order to avoid confusion it is worth noting that present day IGN maps refer to Thiepval Wood as the Bois d' Authuille and the Authuille Wood as Bois de la Haie. In this guide I will **always** refer to these woods by the names used during 1915-18 on the British trench maps which covered this area. The German defences on the north of Thiepval village were known as the Schwaben Redoubt, which overlooked the hamlet of St. Pierre Divion and onwards past the River Ancre towards Beaumont Hamel. Surmounting the spur a little way south west of the village, overlooking Authuille Wood, the German Army had constructed the forbidding Leipzig Redoubt. East of Thiepval the higher ground of Thiepval Ridge spills away past Mouquet Farm in the direction of Courcelette and Martinpuich. The German second line positions running across this ridge, northwards past Mouquet Farm towards Grandcourt, were formidable defences in their own right and were the scene of terribly costly fighting in the autumn of 1916. These areas are within what we can call the designated area of this guide. Before the 'Great Push' many of the British troops were billeted further west in the relative peace of Warloy Baillon, Henencourt, Millencourt, Senlis, Hedauville and Forceville. Throughout the hot early summer of 1916 the British troops would often march east from these small communities, caked in chalk-dust, to undertake their tours of duty in the trenches. Although many casualties of the July 1916 fighting around Thiepval are buried in the cemeteries which abound in these billet villages, these locations familiar to the Tommy of late 1915 and 1916 are not discussed here.

One feature which the young or first time visitor might wish for is an easily accessible reconstruction which gives an insight into the conditions which prevailed around Thiepval at the height of the conflict. The best source of such insight and empathy is to be found at Newfoundland Park, two miles north-west of Thiepval on the Auchonvillers road out of Hamel, the D73. This is an area of preserved battlefield, purchased by the government of Newfoundland after the Great War. Further detailed insight can be obtained at the two quality museums which are within reasonable distance. The first, at Albert below the celebrated Basilica, is only fifteen minutes away by car. The second, the 'Historial' at Peronne, is well worth the longer journey, but you should remember to set aside a good forty minutes travelling time, each way. Take the D938 running south-east from Albert to Peronne, a route which will enable you to follow the southern arm of the British front lines as they existed before the opening of the battle of the Somme.

One extraordinary fact about the Somme and Ancre battlefield is that after the utter devastation of the Great War many of the tracks and other human geographical features were reconstructed in the 1920s with an uncanny similarity to their pre-war locations. Initially the processes of reconstruction were almost insurmountably difficult. One recently demobilized soldier who made an early

Right: Map 1. The Thiepval Battlefield area, showing the pre-war geography of the area. This is taken from the 1;40,000 sheets which accompanied the Official History (1916 Volume 1) which detailed the fighting leading to the first day of the Battle of the Somme.

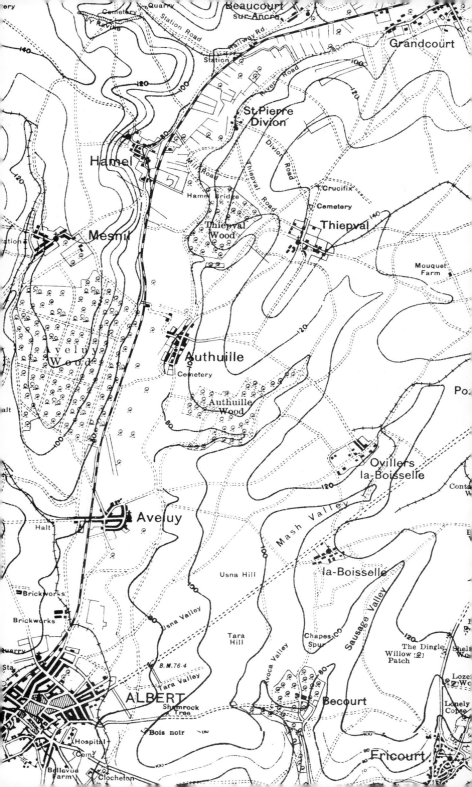

return in the summer of 1919 was the Reverend Major R.H. Royle, M.C., who had fought with the 11th Manchesters at Stuff Redoubt three years earlier. After the war he had exchanged khaki for the cloth, becoming curate of St. Silas the Martyr in Kentish Town, London. This time his journey to the skyline east of Schwaben Redoubt was by car, his purpose to visit old friends who now populated the silent burial grounds which surrounded Thiepval village. On his return he asked, "And what of Thiepval today? A few scarred stumps, a score or more smashed up stones, one solitary civilian grave (alas, how many more graves of our brave laddies) mark the site of what was once a flourishing and contented village. Yet the scene is not without its brighter side. Within a mile of poor, devastated Thiepval, shell holes have been filled in, barbed wire removed and trenches blocked up. Already the French peasants were reaping their harvest, back once more in their own part of their beloved France, living like foxes in holes in the ground, old Nissen huts, trench shelters − anywhere, but full of joy at being home again after nearly five years of exile. At Pozieres a little child was playing on a swing on the top of our old battalion H.Q."[3]

As more villagers returned to rebuild their homes and lives with the reparations monies wrung from Weimar Germany, every effort was made to find the exact location of their pre-war houses. Sometimes, when a villager did not return that plot was left vacant, in many cases still so today! But, we should remember that Thiepval is a working village, a community whose roots are based in centuries of toil on the land which is also our place of interest. This is not 'open access' land on the National Trust model. It is all too easy to let our two interests clash. The foresters in the three nearby woodlands will not take too kindly to an ill considered and noisy intrusion into their domains. During the autumn months, in particular, be aware of the numerous shooting parties. The farmers will not welcome the sight of your tramping the fields with little regard to crops and seeds. Please ask before you enter. Please keep to the paths and the edges of each field.

Thiepval Memorial to the Missing, photographed from the area above Leipzig Redoubt.

HOW TO USE THIS BOOK:

This guide can be used in preparation for your visit, in front of the fire at home on a cold winter evening. In that case it is perhaps best read from start to finish. I think you will have a sound feel for Thiepval at the end of one or two evenings reading and might be ready to book your cross channel ferry for those days in March and April when the weather begins to clear, the fields are ploughed and crop growth has not yet hidden the detail and topography of the ground. But the guide is also designed as a pocket reference, a quick supplement to your knowledge when you are 'walking the course' and need an explanation or clarification.

By far the best way to see the Thiepval area is on foot or bicycle. At the end of the text you can find a number of suggested routes making use of the paths and tracks which are accessible to these means of transport. The chapters dealing with historical events within the designated area are in chronological order. The chapter dealing with cemeteries is constructed in alphabetical order and follows after a description of the memorials which are also identified and described within the same section.

I suggest that a tour by car or coach is the best way to get your sense of bearings and to give an overview of the whole area. Again I have suggested a tour to highlight the main features of the area, along roads which are easily accessible. The roads covered by this suggestion are usually quite satisfactory for coaches and involve no dangerous turns through 360![4] This tour is also to be found at the end of the book and is strongly recommended to those of you not already conversant with the area. It is worth noting that some of the tracks and smaller roads to be found on the IGN maps of the area are not suitable for coaches. Cars without four wheel drive will find difficulty in getting along some minor tracks, for example that leading to the Bouzincourt Ridge cemetery. Be prepared to walk is the best advice that I can give, but do take care to lock all valuables, especially cameras and other inviting items, out of sight in the boot of your vehicle.

LIST OF MAPS

You should note that the trench maps, which are available from the Imperial War Museum Department of Printed Books (tel: 0171 416 5348) or the cartographer of the Western Front Association (members only), follow a specific sequence and should be referred to by the numbers usually found in their top right hand corner. The most useful maps covering the Thiepval area are the 1:10,000 scale sheets as follows: Sheet 57D. S.E. 1&2, entitled Beaumont, (which covers the Thiepval, Mouquet Farm and St Pierre Divion areas, as well as Beaumont Hamel and Beaucourt.) Sheet 57.D. S.E. 4, entitled Ovillers, (which covers the locations immediately south of Thiepval village including the southern tip of Leipzig Redoubt, Authuille Wood and the Blighty Valley areas through to Ovillers.) Variously dated versions are available from both sources. Also very helpful are the 1:5,000 sheets Schwaben redoubt, corrected to 20/10/1916 which covers the area Thiepval to St Pierre Divion with great precision and *Ferme du Mouquet*, corrected to 3/9/1916 and which also covers the Zollern and Stuff redoubts with equal clarity. In the text I have sometimes referred to locations which are noted on trench maps, but not on present day maps. In such cases I have where necessary given the relevant trench map reference to help you identify the exact position.

1. Unfortunately Thiepval lies near the boundary of four of the 1:25,000 IGN maps. Areas to the south of Authuille and Martinsart, including Albert, are covered by 2408 ouest. To complete a set of all the modern 1:25,000 maps covering the area of the British involvement in 'The Battle of the Somme 1916' you should also obtain IGN 2408 est.
2. There are anomalies. Some men's bodies have since been found and are now buried under named headstones. In a small number of cases men are commemorated here at Thiepval even though their deaths occurred away from the Somme area.
3. Published in the Salford City Reporter, 4/10/1919.
4. Where roads are unsuitable for coaches I have mentioned that within the text of the tour routes.

Chapter One
OUR DESIGNATED AREA TODAY

The straight road running from Albert to Bapaume, the D929, neatly bisects what was the British sector of the first Battle of the Somme. However, much of the fighting north of that road in the summer, autumn and early winter of 1916 was influenced by the course of the River Ancre. Today Albert describes itself as being only the *3eme Ville de la Somme*, but quite properly *la Cité d'Ancre*. The Town Hall square in Albert often hosts a market and there are three small supermarkets nearby which can all provide a sound array of food and refreshments. Thiepval is four miles north-north-east of Albert above the east bank of the Ancre, past Authuille Wood at the north-western end of the ridge of higher ground running from Morval, Ginchy and Delville Wood past Pozieres towards Thiepval. Before war visited this region English teas could be had in the village by day trippers seeking the bracing air after a morning's fishing on the river and ponds below. Today the village is devoid of a cafe or restaurant.

The first thing you might therefore need to arrange is accommodation and tomorrow morning's breakfast. Thiepval is not the place to stay in when visiting the area! I have identified below some of the hotels and a number of 'English' B&B style accommodations where you can base yourself during a visit. However, for those of you with a tent or caravan and an adventurous disposition, the 'Bellevue' campsite in Authuille, on the D151, is by far the best and most central point from which to study Thiepval. During 1916 the village defences known as Kintyre Street ran just above the campsite which is just two minutes away from the village of Thiepval by car. The campsite is quiet and often frequented by people who share an interest in the Great War. The owner, Monsieur Desailly, and his family are always welcoming. Recently the Bellevue campsite has been expanded to include a simple restaurant, reached thirty yards to the right of the main campsite entrance, where the food is both substantial and economical. Here you are within two minute's walk of the Authuille Military Cemetery and not far from the Hotel des Pecheurs on the banks of the River Ancre. For many years this hotel, or bar as it is more properly, has served decent food and drinks for as long as you cared to stay! The hotel was sold in 1995 and is now under new management.

However, it can be bitterly cold camping in February! Therefore, for those of you who are travelling in style or during these colder

The Basilica in Albert during 1916, showing the scaffolding which supported the Golden Virgin as she was affectionately known by the 'Tommies'. *Taylor Library*

and wetter months of the year, a roof over your heads may be welcome. The list identified below may be of some help, but it should not be inferred that the order is one of descending merit! To call for reservations from the UK dial 00 33, followed by the 9 digit number. In all these hotels, with one exception in Picquigny, you will find at least one person on the hotel's staff who can speak English.

Hotels

The Royal Picardie***, Route d'Amiens, 80300 Albert.
    Tel 322 75 37 00.
The Hotel de la Basilique**, 3–5 Rue Gambetta, 80300 Albert.
    Tel 322 75 04 71.
The Relais Fleuri**, 56 Avenue Faidherbe, 80300 Albert.
    Tel 322 75 08 11.
The Grande Hotel de la Paix*, 43 Rue Victor Hugo, 80300 Albert.
    Tel 322 75 01 64.
Les Etangs du Levant*, Rue du 1er Septembre, 80340 Bray sur Somme.
    Tel 322 76 70 00.
Auberge de Picquigny**, 112 Rue du 60 R.I., 80310 Picquigny.
    Tel 322 51 20 53.
Hotel Le Prieure, 17 Route National, 80860 Rancourt.
    Tel 322 85 04 43.

B&B style accommodation

Courcelette. A distinctive family farmhouse, self catering or meals provided. Plenty of facilities including guided tours and a small but fascinating museum. This fine location is just ten minutes from Thiepval. Paul Reed and Kieron Murphy, Sommecourt, 39 Grande Rue, 80300 Courcelette. Tel 322 74 01 35.

Auchonvillers/Beaumont Hamel. Very comfortable and well appointed accommodation for up to ten people. Attractive grounds and very interesting walks nearby. Evening meals and continental breakfast. Perhaps ten to fifteen minutes from La Boisselle driving past Newfoundland Park and Thiepval. Mike and Julie Renshaw, Les Galets, Route de Beaumont, Auchonvillers. Tel 322 76 28 79.

Auchonvillers. Five good rooms with en suite facilities and an extremely interesting history, the centrepiece of which is the cellar still carved with the names of many soldiers who passed through in 1916. Bed, breakfast and evening meals by arrangement as well as a Tea Room for non residents. Again, easy access to Thiepval. Avril Williams, 10 Rue Delattre, 80560 Auchonvillers. Tel 322 76 23 66.

Once you are established it is time to see the surrounding locality and I suggest that, soon after you arrive, you would enjoy following the general tour explained in Chapter 7. However, in this first chapter I have attempted to give definition to the boundaries of this guidebook and give a brief commentary to illustrate the importance of the area's history. Whilst you drive it will become clear that the Thiepval plateau or ridge is rather less severe and imposing than some would imagine, given its crucial place in the tactics and strategy of the battles in this area. But in the context of 1914-18 the features are impressive. In some ways the location is not unlike an area of downland in southern England. As with most European chalk uplands there are no sharply defined geological features, simply rolling hills which ebb away into woodlands and the river valley of the Ancre. That river forms the northern limit of this guide as it meanders between Grandcourt and St. Pierre Divion. This was the scene of the last great battle that took place within the Thiepval sector during 1916, the Battle of the Ancre, which was fought out between 13th and the 19th November astride the river between Hamel and Grandcourt. By that time the village of Thiepval had fallen and the British front line enjoyed the advantage of looking down over St. Pierre Divion and Grandcourt from positions north of Schwaben Redoubt and thence eastwards along the Ancre Heights (Stuff Trench past the Stump Road and on into Regina Trench). The Stump Road, running south from Grandcourt and just behind the German second line positions, therefore marks the eastern limits of our designated area.

The largest, by far, of the three main woods at the centre of our area is Aveluy Wood, through which the Albert to Hamel road, the D50, passes. In late 1915 and throughout 1916 Aveluy Wood sheltered many thousands of British soldiers from the German artillery observers located opposite and above them in Thiepval. Today the woods are alive with wildlife, pheasants and deer. The ubiquitous signs, *Propriete Prive* and *Attention ... Pieges* warn all that traps are often set to catch the animals, and to discourage the unwelcome or the unwary. Parties of local people are not averse to using their shotguns in search of game here so be very careful. The inaccessible nature of these woodlands is a pity because the trees and their fallen foliage hide a mass of trenches hurriedly dug above the Amiens to Arras railway line as part of the defences constructed during the spring of 1918. Near the cross roads in Aveluy, where the D50 crosses the D20 Bouzincourt to Aveluy road, a few yards along the road towards Albert, there is a bar where drinks and refreshments can be obtained.

To the west of our designated area, from the villages of Mesnil-Martinsart and along the Bouzincourt ridge behind Aveluy Wood, fine views of the Thiepval battlefield area can be had. Perhaps the best of these viewpoints is at Brock's Benefit (57D SE1 28.d.8,8), a series of artillery observation trenches on the east side of Mesnil, at the head of the communication trench known as Jacob's ladder which ran north-eastwards down the slope from Mesnil into Hamel. Following the general tour will bring you to this location with a sound knowledge of what can then be seen in the panorama to the east and north-east. West of Mesnil and Bouzincourt are the billet villages familiar to the troops as they trained for the forthcoming Battle of the Somme. Even today there are many buildings which witnessed the doings of the Tommies as they prepared and made ready for the forthcoming fight. Here were the estaminets in which a thousand hopes were espoused and a thousand hangovers bought. East of Mesnil the valley of the River Ancre, between Aveluy and Grandcourt, is broad and marshy. In these waterlogged meadows there were few trenches. The engineers spent thousands of hours constructing walkways and repairing bridges to service the needs of the men in the front line trenches below Ovillers and Thiepval. Throughout 1916 it was the unrelenting sport of German artillery units in this area to destroy these valley floor bridges, and the nearby canalized waterways and millraces, in order to flood and disturb the supply routes up to the Authuille area. In some cases the bridges and causeways were named geographically, for example 'northern causeway', in some cases after the Brigadiers whose men they served, 'Jardine' and 'Yatman', and in some cases poetically, 'Black Horse' and the 'Passerelle de Magenta'! Today these broad and watery acres are home to fishing clubs, anglers and their holiday homes.

Still in the centre of our designated area, either side of the village of Authuille, lie two smaller forested areas which the British troops knew as Thiepval and Authuille woods. Whilst the canopy of leaves above the Bois d'Aveluy had remained more or less intact until the late spring of 1916, the woods either side of Authuille had suffered rather more from the impact of shelling and machine gun fire. Both woods still contain extensive evidence of the trench works constructed there during 1914, 1915 and 1916, but again it is advisable to stay on the perimeter of these forested areas for the moment. The beginnings of Authuille Wood can be seen above Blighty Valley cemetery, which is on the left as you travel along the Authuille to Aveluy road, the D151. If you walk along the CWGC path towards Blighty Valley Cemetery you are walking the

The Mill on the Ancre November, 1916. Located south-west of St Pierre Divion at the foot of the Mill Road. See Map 2. *Taylor Library*

The site of the Mill on the Ancre today.

same route as that used by many of the men assembling the night before their anticipated walk across Leipzig Redoubt en route for their assault on the German second line defences north of Mouquet Farm. North-east of Blighty Valley cemetery the lower ground penetrates along what is today known as the Vallee Marceau into the Thiepval plateau or ridge. South east of the valley lies the Ovillers spur, scene of the attacks on 1st July 1916 by the British 8th Division.

On that day the dividing line between the 8th and the 32nd Divisions ran along the floor of Blighty Valley (which was also known to the British as Nab Valley) and continued north-eastwards to a position a few yards south of Mouquet Farm. North of Blighty Valley and Authuille Wood, across that re-entrant from the village of Ovillers la-Boisselle, lies the site of the Leipzig salient. Today its most prominent feature is the quarry and clump of trees, the Granatloch, which identifies the tip of this imposing defensive position. From here it is a short walk along the farmer's track towards the massive memorial which commemorates the British missing and which towers above the landscape here. From within a short distance of the memorial some of the finest views are accessible. Usually it is necessary to walk away from the memorial for a few yards to get the best of the view, but that northwards across the Ancre towards Serre and the northern limits of the 'Great Push' is outstanding.

From the north-eastern face of Thiepval Wood the attack of the 36th (Ulster) Division was launched, across the Mill Road and Thiepval Road on 1st July 1916. Today this is the D73 Thiepval to Hamel road, which was rebuilt in the 1920s on the exact line of the pre 1914 tracks. It is a popular misconception that, because of their pyrrhic success at Schwaben on 1st July, the Ulsters are intrinsically and inextricably linked with the attack on Thiepval village on the opening day of the Battle of the Somme. As we shall see, this is not strictly true. The proposed boundary on the south of the Ulstermen's advance ran from the north-eastern corner of Thiepval Wood, past the village communal cemetery just north of Thiepval and on towards Stuff Redoubt, which lay one mile north-east of the village. Here along the D73 Thiepval Road you can find Connaught Cemetery, the distinctive Mill Road Cemetery and the stark Ulster Memorial Tower. As the Ulstermen swept forward that day many fought their way into the Schwaben Redoubt, on the higher ground above Thiepval village. If you stand on the site of Schwaben Redoubt today, roughly 1,000 yards north-north-east of Thiepval along the D151 at la Grande Ferme,

Map 2. Thiepval trenches according to the British map of the area, late 1915 soon after the arrival of the Ulster Division in this sector, corrected to 2/12/1915. British lines not shown Sheet 57D S.E.1&2 (Parts of).

Author's collection

25

One of the many footbridges spanning the Ancre. This one adjacent to the site of the Mill pictured on page 23. *Taylor Library*

you can discover the most complete panorama of the northern 'Somme' battlefield and look down north-westwards to the northern limit of our designated area at St. Pierre Divion in the Ancre Valley. Here, in the watery and fouled marshes of 1916, there were no trenches around the old mill just east of Hamel. Across and north-west of the river here lies Beaumont Hamel[1] which is outside the scope of this volume.

In the centre of our area lies Thiepval village. On the outbreak of war it was the site of some sixty homes comprising more than ninety buildings in all. Thiepval was identified as the sixth largest of the Somme battlefield villages. By the late summer of 1916 not one of those family homes remained standing. On the morning of 1st July 1916 the village was the scene for a tragic and futile frontal attack by Salford and Tyneside battalions. Today the vicinity has a different significance, as a place of pilgrimage for many people whose family life and circumstances have been shaped and altered by the events of eighty years past, here on the Somme. The cemetery beneath the towering memorial is a joint Anglo-French burial ground, symbolizing the co-operation and partnership between the British Empire and French forces. However, the enormity and significance of the memorial determines that the bulk of the visitors will have crossed the channel from the United Kingdom, in many cases following the same route as the generations who fought and died here in such prodigal numbers during 1916 and 1918.

Running south-east from Thiepval is the road leading to Pozieres, the D73. Looking along that road from the Thiepval Memorial to the Missing the present day Mouquet Farm can be clearly seen, just over a mile away. On 1st July 1916 it was one of the second objectives to the 32nd Division's men and was expected to fall to them within one hour and forty minutes of the attack starting! One hour later the third objectives including Goat Redoubt (Feste Zollern) and Stuff Redoubt (Feste Staufen) on the main German second line defences were also expected to fall. In fact these locations were the subject of massively ferocious and costly fighting, involving the 11th and 18th Divisions in late September 1916, all of fourteen weeks later! That was the Battle of Thiepval Ridge, which itself followed terribly costly fighting in the Ovillers and Pozieres areas, culminating in the Battle of Flers — Courcelette between 15th and 22nd September. The final episodes in the fighting for the high ground overlooking Grandcourt took place during the Battle of the Ancre Heights on 21st October and later within the Ancre Valley in early November. Present to witness and record the atmosphere and tragedy of the war throughout those terrible weeks was Edmund Blunden, author of *Undertones of War*, whose literature and poetry details the fighting around Schwaben Redoubt and along the Ancre Heights with great clarity, imagery and sensitivity.

The southern limits of our designated area are therefore along a line drawn from the village of Aveluy, past the south of Authuille Wood and on towards Mouquet farm. As a rule of thumb this is generally a line parallel with the Albert to Bapaume road, one mile to the north of that road. It is worth noting that the area south and east of Mouquet Farm, including the villages of Pozieres and Courcelette, will be the subject of a further volume in this series.

1. The area of Beaumont Hamel, and in particular Newfoundland Park, is the subject of another volume in the Battleground Europe series (Nigel Cave, 1994).

Chapter Two
THE GERMAN POSITIONS

Within weeks of the outbreak of war the German Army was positioned on the heights overlooking Authuille village. Their arrival on the misty morning of 27th September 1914 had marked a tragedy for the Vaquette family who lived in Authuille. Boromee Vaquette was shot by French soldiers who had mistaken him for the German troops they sought. The first Frenchman to die in the war in this area was therefore killed by the rifles of his own countrymen. The French troops were devastated by their error. Boromee's body was recovered by the same troops one week later and is buried in the family plot of the communal cemetery. The village of Authuille quickly became uninhabitable and the civilian population moved to friends and relatives in Albert and Amiens. The chateau at Thiepval began its decline into weed-ridden and shell-torn devastation.

Whilst many French units opposed them during the first eight months of 1915, the German soldiers who occupied the Thiepval sector, all belonging to units of the 26th Reserve Division, were thoroughly used to the location and its geography. That division's sector ran from Ovillers to Beaumont Hamel. Their positions were a natural and formidable defensive situation. Thiepval's height, and the exposed slopes of many of the approaches, meant that any attacking force would be immediately under a disadvantage. In fact there was little fighting here and a policy of 'live and let live' had been expeditiously adopted by both sides. The British only arrived within this previously 'cushy' sector in the autumn of 1915. From nowhere in the British sector was the higher land east of Thiepval capable of being observed. Almost all of the front line defences at Thiepval were manned by the 99th Reserve Infantry Regiment (99 RIR). These units were comprised of soldiers who had fought in the early engagements of the war and who had then, as the front settled into a static and relatively undisturbed trench routine, set about the task of fortifying Thiepval throughout almost twenty months of occupancy, until July 1916. By that time their divisional artillery had ranged almost every known location in the British sector opposite. The German soldiers knew the area intimately. Hailing from Wurttemberg they were a determined and proud regiment.

By early 1916 the British sector opposite the 99 RIR was occupied by three divisions, the 32nd, 36th and 49th. On 1st July the initial assault would be entrusted to the 32nd and 36th Divisions. The

The chateau at Thiepval as it was before war visited the area in 1914.

A German soldier's photograph of the Chateau from the village church, spring 1915.

The walled pond which marked the village centre prior to its devastation by shell fire. Today there is no trace of this pond.

The German front line trench system in early 1915 viewed from the area of Thiepval Chateau, looking north.

This diagrammatic representation of the Thiepval area shows the view from an imaginary balloon flying behind the German lines facing towards the British positions below Thiepval. Although it cannot be a perfect reconstruction of the land, woods and fortifications, it may help you visualize the situation within which the British troops found themselves during the spring of 1916.

David Kelsall

KEY: 1. Bouzincourt; 2. Martinsart; 3. Mensil; 4. Englebelmer; 5. Mailly-Maillet; 6. Auchonvillers; 7. Mary Redan; 8. Railway gully in No Man's Land; 9. German Front Line (1st July); 10. Hamel; 11. Mill on Ancre; 12. Thiepval Wood; 13. Authuille; 14. Authuille Wood; 15. Aveluy; 16. Thiepval; 17. Schwaben Redoubt; 18. Wonder Work; 19. Jacob's Ladder; 20. St Pierre Divion (out of sight below hill); 21. German Front Line (1st July); 22. British Front Line (1st July); 23. Aveluy Wood; 24. Thiepval Chateau.

32nd were a broad mixture of Regular and New Army battalions from Enniskillen in Ireland, the Highlands and Lowlands of Scotland, Dorsetshire, Lancashire, the Lakeland areas, Yorkshire and Northumberland. Alongside the left of the 32nd Division would be the 36th Division, within which almost every infantryman was an Ulster loyalist volunteer, positioned a little to the north-west of Thiepval opposite the German sub-sectors known as C4, C3, C2 and C1 and on past the Ancre marshes towards Beaumont Hamel. All along this frontage, with the brief exception of the land adjacent to the marshes between St. Pierre Divion and Hamel, the German trenches overlooked the British lines by a height difference of at least sixty five feet. No Man's Land, the gap between the front lines, was on average two hundred and fifty yards in front of the British 32nd Division's sector and four hundred yards in front of the 36th Division. In that No Man's Land on the right of the 99 RIR's sector, that is in front of 36th (Ulster Division), the gap between the lines was neatly bisected by the Thiepval Road which then led onto the Mill Road running down to the River Ancre.

Opposite below left: A German infantryman poses in front of his home before leaving with his regiment for the Thiepval area.

Opposite below right: Thiepval church, 1915, below which a well is accessed from within the trench system.

Below: A German staff officer of the 26th Reserve Division in the trenches, believed to be at St Pierre Divion church, during early 1915.

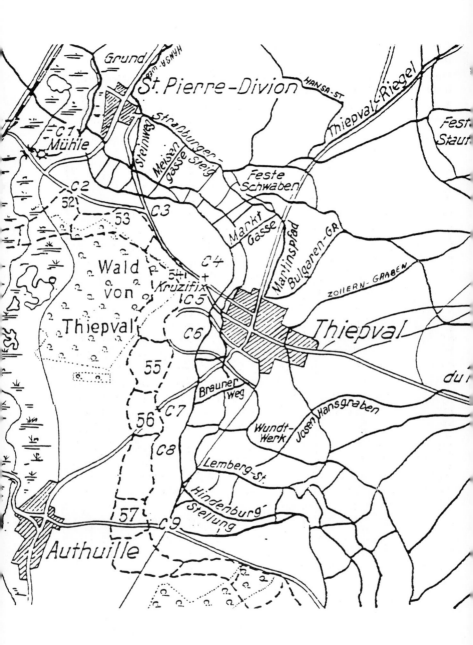

Map 3. The German defences, July 1916, including the main redoubts, with trenches identified using their correct German titles.

The 99th Reserve Infantry Regiment's sector ran from the banks of the Ancre at St. Pierre Divion along to the tip of the Leipzig Redoubt or Granatloch. As we have seen, their trench lines were numbered into sub-sectors, C1 adjacent to the Ancre along to C9 at Leipzig Redoubt. This entire sector was comprised of three sections, each section being held by one battalion. These three battalion sections were Thiepval-North (C1 to C3), Thiepval-Middle or Central (C4 to C6) and Thiepval-South to C9. Three companies would hold the front line whilst a fourth would be held in reserve, nearby. The 99th Reserve Infantry Regiment was distinct from some other German regiments in that it was composed of four battalions rather than the normal three, the fourth being placed as a Corps reserve and later as the reserve for the 26 Reserve Division. The regiment had two machine gun companies whose guns covered the entirety of their regiment's front here at Thiepval. Twenty-five guns were available by July 1st 1916, including one captured Russian weapon and one British.

Whilst this German position was already a strong one, it was made almost impregnable following the arrival of Major von Fabeck on April 15th, 1916. Von Fabeck was a meticulous soldier who had previously commanded the Guard Jager Battalion in the Vosges mountains. He was the nephew of Field Marshal Paul von Hindenburg. On the day of his arrival Von Fabeck inspected the entirety of his new regimental sector and issued immediate orders for the improvement of the defences. Each dugout, were it not already done, should be deepened to 7 metres, with three exits. These dugouts were to be clustered into groups of three, each cluster's dugouts connected by tunnels. Complexes capable of housing large bodies of men were to be built, each sunk 8-10 metres deep and with multiple exits. The largest, at St. Pierre Divion, was capable of housing 1,000 men. It was constructed near the south bank of the Ancre under the shelter of the clay embankment south-west of the hamlet of St. Pierre Divion. In the embankment there were four main entrances running back towards the main shelters. Stairways connected the shelters with the trenches above and further exits were available from tunnels sunk eastwards towards Schwaben Redoubt and the German front lines north and east of Thiepval Wood. There were a number of ventilation shafts. The area beneath Schwaben contained hospital accommodation as well as officers quarters and numerous shelters capable of housing sections of troops. A smaller shelter, at Mouquet Farm, housed 300 men. Mouquet Farm was the site of 99 RIR battle headquarters and the new shelter there provided

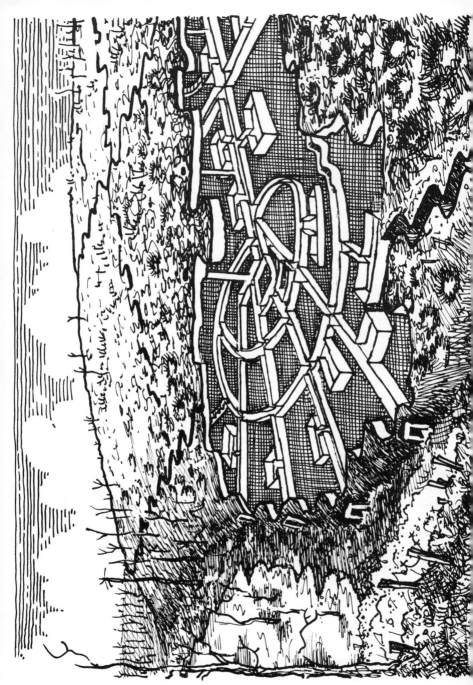

A diagram to show the system of underground protection constructed between St. Pierre Divion and the Schwaben Redoubt. *David Kelsall*

accommodation for the headquarters staff, a telephone exchange, water supply and pumping equipment as well as medical and rest facilities. The pumping facilities at Mouquet Farm carried water forward from the water station at Courcelette which had been constructed on the site of the sugar refinery[1]. Both the St. Pierre Divion and Mouquet Farm complexes were completed on June 23rd 1916.

Von Fabeck's thoroughness also extended to the above ground defences and communication systems. The two machine gun company commanders were instructed to find premier positions for each of their guns, giving the best fields of fire. They were also entrusted with the task of identifying alternative sites for each weapon in case those were needed if forward positions were located by the British artillery and therefore made unusable. The forward trenches west of the village in front of the chateau, known as Thiepval Fort, were organized to provide the machine gun teams with interlocking fields of fire. These guns could sweep the upper parts of Thiepval spur, in front of Thiepval Wood, as well as providing enfilade fire to the south down the Authuille road and across No Man's Land on the west of Leipzig Salient. Additional lamp and flag signalling stations were constructed and further telephone cables were buried 2 metres below the floor of each trench. The complexity of the defences was aided by the addition of new communication trenches and the deepening and strengthening of the already existent trenches. All along the Thiepval sector the German front lines were to a depth of three sequential fire trenches. At the rear of the third fire trench, the German reserve line, lay the two important flank fortifications which protected Thiepval, the Schwaben Redoubt *Feste Schwaben* on the higher ground north of the village and the *Wundt-Werk* (or Wonder Work on contemporary British maps) to the south, just above Leipzig Redoubt.

Feste Schwaben lay 700 yards north of Thiepval, alongside the Thiepval to Grandcourt Road. It occupied the north-western shoulder of the Thiepval Ridge and overlooked and supported the German positions within St. Pierre Divion, and across the valley at Beaucourt-sur-Ancre and Beaumont Hamel. On the north towards the banks of the Ancre, north-east towards Battery Valley and Grandcourt, west towards Thiepval Wood and south-west along the Authuille Road the land sloped away from Feste Schwaben with a noticeable steepness unusual in this area. It was regarded by both sides as an imposing location. Its great complex of trenches, command posts, telephone exchanges and underground shell-proof

A medium Minenwerfer trench mortar team with their gun. *Whitehead*

shelters dominated the ground onto which the British troops would debouch from their assembly positions in Thiepval Wood and the land across which the Ulstermen would have to attack on 1st July. This was the tactical key to the defence of the Thiepval Ridge. If the *Feste Schwaben* could be taken by the British, then Thiepval village would be exposed to an attack on equal terms from the north and would therefore become vulnerable from that direction.

Seven hundred yards south of the village and its chateau stood the *Wundt-Werk*, above the Leipzig Salient on the trench known as *Hohenzollern Stellung*. Its position lay slightly to the reverse of the Thiepval spur in order to give protection from directly observed artillery fire. It was less imposing than the *Feste Schwaben*,, recognition that Schwaben was the most significant of these two flank positions. However, south-west of and protecting the forward face of the *Wundt-Werk* lay a series of massively fortified trenches in a sequence running down the spur, *Turken Stellung*, *Lemberg*

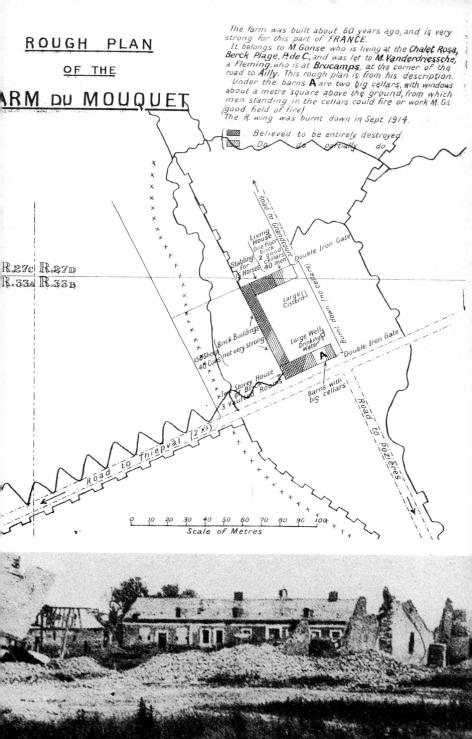

ROUGH PLAN

OF THE

ARM DU MOUQUET

The farm was built about 60 years ago, and is very strong for this part of FRANCE.

It belongs to M Gonse who is living at the Chalet Rosa, Berck Plage, P. de C., and was let to M. Vanderdriessche, a Fleming, who is at Brucamps, at the corner of the road to Ailly. This rough plan is from his description.

Under the barns A are two big cellars, with windows about a metre square above the ground, from which men standing in the cellars could fire or work M.Gs. (good field of fire)

The R. wing was burnt down in Sept. 1914.

▨ Believed to be entirely destroyed.
▧ Do   do   partially   do

R.27c R.27d
R.33a R.33b

Road to Grandcourt

Living House
One floor
brick
2 good
cellars
40 men

Stabling for Horses

Double Iron Gate

Large Cistern

Burnt down (no cellars)

Large Well Drinking Water

A

Double Iron Gate

Brick Buildings not very strong

150 Sheep 40 Cows

Barns with big cellars

1 Storey House of Brick
3 Vaulted Rooms

Road to Pozières

Road to Thiepval (2 K's)

0 10 20 30 40 50 60 70 80 90 100
Scale of Metres

Stellung, Hindenburg Stellung and the very front line positions of the Granatloch or quarry. At the tip of that salient those German front lines turned sharply, running east for half a mile into Blighty or Nab Valley, before continuing south towards Ovillers-la-Boisselle.

Although the fortifications described above were the most significant in the front line positions, other locations are worthy of note. St. Pierre Divion, apart from housing many reserves in the shelters built underground there, was an important and strongly entrenched position in its own right, guarding the gap in the trench lines created by the water meadows and marshes of the Ancre river. The slopes running up towards *Feste Schwaben* above St. Pierre Divion were enfiladed by the many machine guns located in *Feste Alt Wurttemberg*, the Beaucourt Redoubt, just north-west of Beaucourt sur Ancre on the northern bank of the river. The rear of Thiepval village was a further powerfully developed position, as was the *Nordwerk* which lay within the 8th Division's objectives on 1st July. The *Nordwerk* lay roughly one mile east of the tip of Leipzig Salient, some five hundred yards behind the German front line trenches opposite the Nab.

One mile or more to the rear of their front line positions around Thiepval the Germans had constructed a very strong second line position. This was effectively a line running North-north-west from the fortified village of Pozieres to Grandcourt through a series of redoubts at Mouquet Farm, Goat Redoubt (*Feste Zollern*) and Stuff Redoubt (*Feste Staufen*). A long intermediate trench for evacuation and re-enforcement purposes connected Schwaben Redoubt with Mouquet Farm, this was known as the Mouquet Switch line. A similar intermediate line left Schwaben in the direction of Grandcourt, the Hansa Line. A number of other communication trenches running from west to east connected the German front lines with their second line positions. These parallel trenches would become central in the fighting for Thiepval which occurred during the September to November period of 1916.

In the relatively quiet period which had developed in this area during 1915, and throughout the rather more trying early months of 1916, Thiepval could be said to have exerted great influence over the conduct of operations in this area. Because of its imposing location no amount of offensive spirit on the part of newly arrived New Army British troops had been able to gain an ascendancy over the German troops occupying the high ground in this area. Consequently the defences had been able to grow in strength and depth. Thiepval was, by June 1916, equipped as the strong right arm of the German defences along the high ground astride the Albert to Bapaume Road. This upland area was crucial in that it protected the great railhead of Bapaume. The Thiepval sector held by 99 RIR also happened to be, geographically, almost centrally located within the battle-front chosen by Haig as the launchpad of his summer offensive. This was the 'Great Push' which many Tommies and their inexperienced and often naive officers thought, with misplaced optimism, would end the war. All the combatant's staff were aware that the prize of Thiepval was a vital one. British success here would enable observation and dominance of the battlefield to the north as well as threatening the higher ground across the Albert to Bapaume road. The German resolve was therefore immensely deep and determined here. Every attempt on the part of the British to gain ascendancy was always matched by retribution. A moving example was that suffered by the Dorsets, in early May, for whom the month became a trying and dangerous period in front of Thiepval.

A light Minenwerfer trench mortar team with their gun. *Whitehead*

The site of Hammerhead Sap today (see 'X' on map opposite which indicates the photographer's viewpoint).

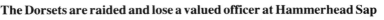

The Dorsets are raided and lose a valued officer at Hammerhead Sap

The location of these events surrounding Hammerhead are easily accessible from the D73 west of Thiepval village.

On the night of the 5/6th May the 15th Lancashire Fusiliers (1st Salford Pals) had raided the German trenches opposite.[2] A further raid by the 36th Division had also been planned for the night of the 7/8th and it was coincidental that on that same night the predictable German reply to the earlier Salford's raid was delivered, in devastating fashion, at the junction between the 32nd and 36th Division's positions near Hammerhead Sap. Fortunately for the Salfords they were not the recipients of that retribution. At just thirty minutes before midnight on 6th May the 1st Dorsets had relieved the 1st Salford Pals in the line in the Thiepval subsector. The following night, at 11.00 pm, the German artillery opened a very heavy bombardment on the whole of the Dorset's lines. C and D Companies were in the front line fire trench. By this time the Ulster raiding party, from the 9th Inniskillings, were out in No Man's Land and about to enter the German trenches west of Schwaben Redoubt. The German barrage started around the head of Hamilton Avenue, east of Caterpillar Wood, along to the Maison Grise sap at Thiepval Point South but then gradually shifted north and fell heavily around the Hammerhead Sap position. By 11.15 this fire had become intense with trench mortars directed on the front lines and field guns and howitzers trained on the support and communication trenches of Sauchiehall Street,

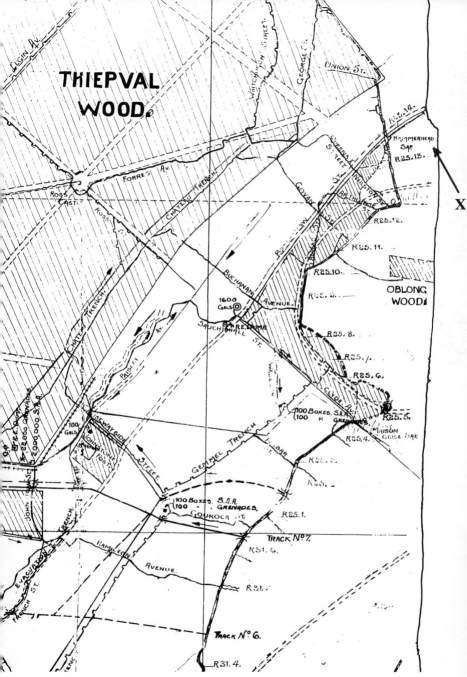

Map 4. The site of the German raid on the 1st Dorset's positions on the night of 7th/8th May, 1916.

Buchanan Avenue, Govan Street, Queens Cross Street and the north-east end of Paisley Avenue.

At half past eleven three parties of Germans attacked D Company's positions on the left of the Dorset's line, most of which had now been badly damaged by the trench mortar bombs and artillery fire. One group of Germans feinted towards the right of the Dorsets positions, exiting Diamond Wood and heading towards Maison Grise sap. Another stronger party of Germans left Oblong Wood and entered the Dorset's lines near Thiepval Point North and bombed their way north in the direction of Hammerhead Sap. A third group briefly entered the Hammerhead Sap but were quickly driven out. In that process the Dorsets received considerable help from the Derry Volunteers, the 10th Royal Inniskilling Fusiliers. By the time the raiders had been forced out much damage had nevertheless been done. The Dorsets suffered one officer killed, one wounded, together with twelve men killed, twenty-eight wounded, twenty-four missing together with a number of cases of 'shell shock' and the after effects of gas inhalation. The men killed during this raid are buried in Authuille Military Cemetery.

The recriminations amongst the brigade and battalion staff were bitter after these events, much paperwork being issued to identify

This photograph shows the Dorsets' 'missing' being held in the nearby village of Grandcourt, by their German captors, after the raid on 7th/8th May, 1916. *Whitehead*

Troops observe from British positions below Thiepval. *Taylor Library*

the blameworthy for what had happened! However, little was learned and the most extraordinary lapse would take place ten days later.[3] On 16th May Captain William Algeo had been out from Hammerhead Sap, quite contrary to standing orders and 'in direct disobedience of repeated orders on the subject' but 'smoking his pipe quite cool', and walked towards the German positions. Perhaps morale was not at its best in the 1st Dorsets following the earlier German raid, certainly that day there were two 'self inflicted wounds' amongst men serving with that battalion. It was almost certainly the case that Captain Algeo was trying to re-establish a confident and offensive spirit amongst his men since he was, by all accounts, an indefatigable and fearless soldier who had longer experience of trench warfare than any other in the battalion at that time. The following day two officers, Captain Algeo again, but this time accompanied by Lieutenant Henry Mansel-Pleydell, who was the battalion's Intelligence Officer, left the tip of Hammerhead Sap and entered the shrub-land beyond in broad daylight at 11.30 am. The two officers were seen running into the trees after which shouting was heard and many shots rang out. It was clear that no rescue could be considered since all the advantage lay with the German patrols within the wooded area beyond Hammerhead. To investigate the situation the pioneer sergeant, Sergeant W. Goodwillie, together with Sergeant Rogers, were allowed to go out. After the sound of further shooting only Sergeant Rogers returned and it could only have been hoped that the other three were taken as Prisoners of War. In fact all three had been killed and the matter soon came under the scrutiny of a Court of Enquiry. It was a matter of considerable embarrassment to a Regular battalion that recklessness had led to the needless loss of experienced and crucial figures. The two officers, together with Sergeant Goodwillie, are buried at Miraumont Communal Cemetery extension.

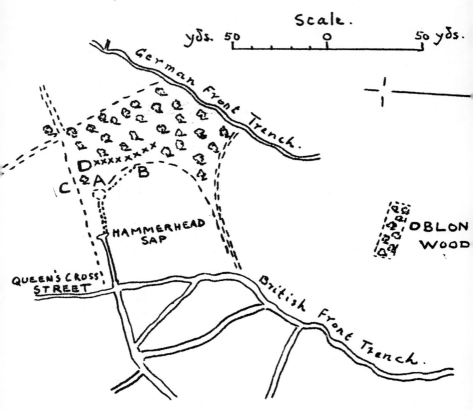

Map 5. This map accompanied the battalion report on the loss of Captain Algeo and his comrades. It shows the point at which the two officers entered the shrub-land (B), Sergeant Goodwillie was seen by Rogers to get to point D before the two sergeants lost contact. It is worth noting that today all of this area which was wooded and shrub covered has since been ploughed up leaving the area which was originally the chateau gardens now bare for crops. The trench map reference for Hammerhead Sap is Sheet 59 D, SE 1&2 (parts of) R.25.a.6,3.

Sometimes the days and detail of trench warfare were whittled down to the observation of the smallest and most mundane matters. Charles Douie, who was serving with the Dorsets during this period, recorded an image of the Thiepval trenches which:

'ran through the garden of Thiepval Chateau, and in the absence of shell fire there was much that was attractive in the view over the valley of the Ancre and the woods of Thiepval, Aveluy and Authuille on each side, now beautiful in the glory of spring. Flowers were often to be found growing in the sides of the trenches and in No Man's Land, and just below my dug-out there were the remains of two red-brick gateposts which had led from the chateau garden to the orchard in the valley below. The flowers found their way into dug-outs; the orchard was swept by machine guns night and day, and if the apple trees bore any fruit in 1916 there was no one so foolhardy as to seek it. I was sitting one morning in my dug-out overlooking the orchard when I witnessed a strange little comedy. I was growing drowsy; we had been through a time of great strain. Our trenches had been destroyed by a barrage of great intensity; the Germans had attacked, and there had been heavy fighting with bomb and bayonet in our lines. Now there was a lull. The sun was warm, and a breeze whispered in the shell-riven trees. There was no sound of war but the intermittent thud of a sniper's bullet from the ruins of the chateau as it struck the earth. I was nearly asleep when my eye was caught by a most unwarlike scene in the entrance to the dug-out. A dud shell lay partly embedded in the dry mud. A mouse with his head on one side peered at me, then took refuge behind the shell, reappearing a moment later on the far side. This was repeated several times. Then, emboldened, the mouse departed and brought back a friend. A game ensued, and whenever I blinked the two mice fell over each other in a ludicrously human way as they sought the security of their strange haven.[4]'

At the other end of the scale of magnitude the massive preparations being undertaken behind the British lines were a certain indication of impending action. After 26th May the Germans noted a number of captive balloons which were visible from their Thiepval positions, one opposite Hebuterne, one behind Mesnil, one north and two south of Albert. Lively labour behind the British front lines was noted, the unloading of rails, iron gas bottles, heavy beams, wire spools and the movement of columns of infantry and ammunition trains. The 99 RIR's men were in a state of constant tension and readiness.

47

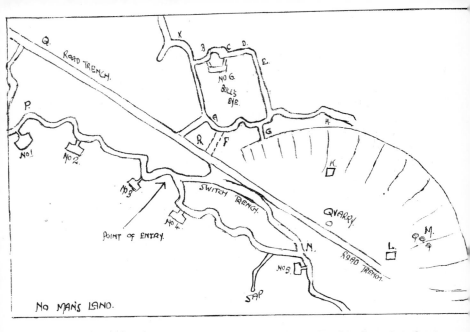

Map 6. Sketch map produced by the Lonsdales showing the point of entry into the German trenches to the west and north of Authuille Quarry.

The Lonsdales raid the Granatloch in search of vital intelligence

The location of this raid, undertaken just one month after that suffered by the Dorsets, is easily visualized today from the position of the farmer's track which runs north westwards from the quarry towards the D151, across the fields identified on the IGN 1:25000 Bapaume ouest sheet as *les Couturelles*. The German trenches east of the Thiepval track and just a few yards north of the quarry or Granatloch were known as 'The Bull's Eye'.

On the night of the 5/6th June the 11th Border (Lonsdale) battalion undertook an important raid here whose purpose was to obtain prisoners and to explore the German defences at the north end of the Granatloch. This, and the many similar raids being conducted along the intended battle-front, should have provided an adequate picture of the state of German defence in this area. The raid was launched from the head of a communication trench opposite Authuille Quarry, Tyndrum Street located at R.31.c.10.46. Because this quarry, the Granatloch, was on a reverse slope incapable of direct observation the Lonsdale's way forward was identified by a huge white arrow laid out behind their positions and directed at the point of entry. The accuracy of that direction was confirmed by spotter planes, although that almost certainly meant that the Germans opposite were also forewarned. On the night of the raid the process of maintaining direction was aided by the laying of tapes in No Man's Land within which the raiders would confine their outward and return movements. The raid was led by Lieutenant William Barnes and consisted of four officers, twenty-four NCOs and fifty-five men.

Soon after 11pm the raiders were formed up in No Man's Land and the British bombardment had begun. The German artillery retaliated swiftly and, as the raiders approached the German front lines at 11.10 pm, those trenches themselves came under a heavy German bombardment directed from their second line positions. After groups using Bangalore torpedoes had cleared the German wire the Lonsdale's raiding party entered the German positions at 11.17 pm., and the process of taking prisoners, clearing the dugouts and mapping the defences began. Crosses marking a number of German graves were identified near to the southern end of the quarry. The problem of 'conducting' the unfortunate prisoners back to the British line was, however, severe:

'Five of the prisoners whom it was found difficult to bring over were killed by their conductors on the way. These prisoner conductors had to pass thro' the German barrage on No Man's Land which was very heavy at the time, and they found themselves compelled to dispose of these Germans to prevent the possibility of their escape.'[5]

On attempting to return Lieutenant Barnes and three men were killed in No Man's Land by the German barrage. However, apart from identifying that the earth was smashed by artillery fire the surviving raiders were also able to detail the many dugouts which abounded in the area. All were intact and were identified as having floors about twenty-two feet below ground level!

Armed with such specific detail, and watching during the last week of June as the enormous preliminary bombardment fired by the British artillery systematically searched Thiepval, there was great hope in the mind of the British X Corps' Commanding Officer, Lieutenant-General Morland, that Thiepval and the Schwaben Redoubt would prove vulnerable. Certainly the barbed wire was known to be thoroughly cut in many places north of Thiepval but the reality was that the cellars of the villager's houses provided shelter against all but the direct hit of a large calibre howitzer round. The crumbled brickwork absorbed the shock of shellfire and protected Thiepval's occupants. The 36th Division's diary noted that:

'on the 26th there was a concentrated bombardment from 9

<u>Description of Dugouts.</u>

The five dugouts in the front line were all of the same type, as shewn in sketch below. The entrance in each case under the parapet. The interior walls of the dugouts and passages were boarded, and the floors duckboarded. There we ten steps down to each dugout, the floors of which were abou 14' below the level of the bottom of the trench.

Dugout in Front Trench.

Short passage blocked after a few feet.

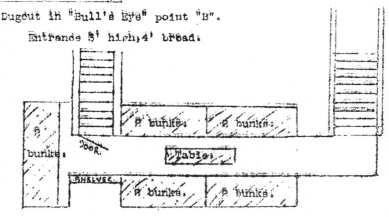

<u>Information (Continued):</u>

Dugout in "Bull's Eye" point "B".

Entrance 3' high, 4' broad.

The sketches of the dugouts which were located by the Lonsdales during their raid of the Granatloch and surrounding positions on the night of 5/6th June 1916.

till 10.20 a.m. on the West end of Thiepval in which all natures of artillery took part. The Chateau and West portion of the village were reduced to ruins, but the enemy's trench mortars and machine guns continued to give trouble on succeeding days and calls to silence them were constantly given to the British artillery.'[6]

One German letter, written at this time by Unteroffizier Hinkel of the 7th Company 99 RIR, described his men's feelings under the stress of this barrage. 'Seven long days of artillery fire without a break, that in itself still more heightened the effect of the barrage's violence. In addition, on the 27th and 28th June, gas on our trench. The torment and fatigue are unspeakable, only competing with the strain on the nerves. Merely a prayer in our hearts, "Lord, release the pressure in us, give us escape through battle, give us victory; Lord God! Allow the Englishman finally to come", and the desire grew with each successive fall of shell.'[7] The machine gun nests which Von Fabeck had so carefully sited had not been found, and on the day of the assault all would be capable of being brought into action.

Officer and men of a Maxim machine gun team at Thiepval. *Whitehead*

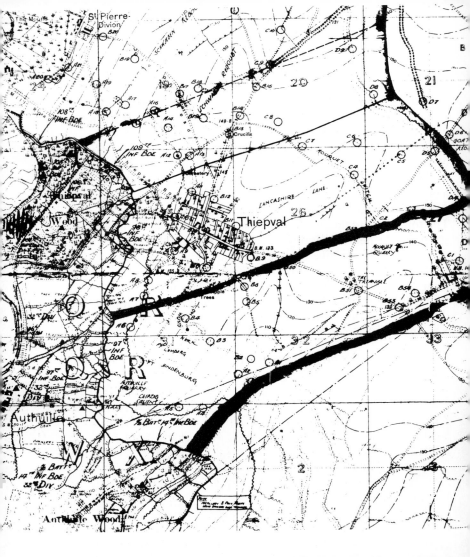

Map 7. Planning and deployment of the 32nd and 36th Divisions before their attacks on Thiepval on 1st July, 1916.

1. Today those tunnels originate under the lifting rig at the garden centre at Courcelette.
2. See *Salford Pals*, Stedman
3. See 14 Brigade War Diary, P.R.O. WO 95/2389, and *A Sergeant Major's War*, Shephard (who was serving within the 1st Dorsets at this time). Crowood Press 1987.
4. Charles Douie, *The Weary Road*
5. 97 Brigade War Diary, WO 95/2399
6. 36th Division's War Diary, WO 95/2491
7. *In the Hurricane of the Somme* The history of 99 RIR

Chapter Three
THE BRITISH PERSPECTIVE TO JULY 1916

As we have already noted the German Army had identified, occupied and clinically fortified the most favourable positions above the banks of the Ancre at Thiepval. From the British perspective that meant that any attack in this area would be undertaken uphill. If you stand on the road looking from Thiepval village down towards the eastern face of Thiepval Wood the unprotected nature of that uphill struggle can be easily visualized. The slope is gradual and open. In the last one hundred metres of any advance those men attacking the village would be totally exposed. The view north-west from Thiepval across the north-eastern face of Thiepval Wood is equally unobstructed. The glacis was and is bare of any cover.

However, there was great optimism and pride amongst the men being assembled in this area and whose task it would be to take Thiepval and the surrounding positions. The three divisions under the command of X Corps contrasted sharply in both their origins and character.[1] The 49th Division was a Territorial Force from the West Riding of Yorkshire. They took no part in the initial assault on 1st July and their subsequent deployment later in the day was marked by indecision and had little impact. The 32nd Division, which would be the right hand division of X Corps' attack, were rather typical of many of the mainland New Army divisions raised by Kitchener. Each of the three brigades was strengthened, or 'stiffened' in the curt phrase of that period, by one regular battalion. The other units in each brigade were service battalions raised soon after the outbreak of war from communities in northern England and Scotland.

The 36th Division however was unique.

It was one of the three divisions raised in Ireland, the 10th (Irish), the 16th (Irish) and the 36th (Ulster) Divisions. In the catastrophic and depressing chronicle of Ireland's recent history the story of the Ulstermen's assault at Thiepval has become legendary. Its roots lay in the turbulent issues of nationalism and loyalist opposition. In the months immediately before the outbreak of war the question of Home Rule had polarized those opinions and heightened tension in Ireland. In the north, inspired by Sir Edward Carson, a volunteer force of loyalists had joined together to make plain their implacable opposition to the proposed legislation which they believed would undermine their position as 'citizens of the UK'. These volunteers soon became an army of

80,000 men under the command of General Sir George Richardson, the Ulster Volunteer Force, whose public displays of drilling and massed ranks were a great embarrassment to Asquith's British Government. But the outbreak of war saw a temporary cessation of the interminable Irish issue and Kitchener seized the opportunity to negotiate with Carson for his help in raising another Irish unit. The order for the formation of the 36th Division was issued on 28th October 1914. The task was enormously simplified by the existence of the UVF's administrative structure. The battalions were made up from the communities of Northern Ireland and mirrored the UVF's formations, the Belfast Volunteers, Antrim, County Down, Armagh, Monaghan, Cavan, Tyrone, Derry, Donegal and Fermanagh. The 36th Division's commanding officer was Major General Oliver Nugent, who was exceptionally proud of the men under his command. His division had arrived in France during October 1915. Unlike many other New Army divisions the Ulstermen were not divided and split up in the weeks after they left the UK in order to allow a stiffening of regulars. Here then was an Irish Loyalist division of work-place friends, like-minded and now determined to demonstrate and uphold their fierce adherence to the crown. How extraordinary that in the months which preceded the war these men had been preparing to fight against the forces of the crown!

The objectives which had been identified to these two assault divisions made clear that a deep penetration of the German positions was expected. The 36th Division faced a difficulty in that their final objectives on the German second positions fanned out into a much wider frontage than that facing the initial assault across the front lines. Therefore, the original plan of attack devised by Nugent's 36th Division did not envisage a frontal attack on Schwaben from the west across Thiepval Road but was to attack St. Pierre Divion directly and then the slopes leading up to the Schwaben Redoubt from the north-west, thereby avoiding the effects of machine gun fire from Thiepval fort should that village not fall to the 32nd Division.[2] However, although this plan had already been rehearsed it was abandoned at the request of Major-General Rycroft, GOC 32nd Division, who believed that it would not deliver sufficient support to his men attacking Thiepval. As a consequence the Ulstermen's attack was moved right, leaving St. Pierre Divion to be surrounded and pinched out later.

It was anticipated that all the way along the Thiepval front the 36th and 32nd Divisions would be in possession of the German second line defences, the 'D' lines, roughly 2,000 yards to the rear

This diagrammatic image of the Thiepval area shows the view from an imaginary balloon flying behind the British lines looking towards the German positions around Thiepval. Although it cannot be a perfect reconstruction of the land and fortifications, this will help you visualize the situation of the village, the surrounding features and the direction of the many assaults which were being planned.   David Kelsall

KEY: 1. Grandcourt; 2. Stuff Redoubt; 3. Goat Redoubt; 4. Schwaben Redoubt; 5. Crucifix; 6. St Pierre Divion; 7. Thiepval Wood; 8. Mill/Bridge on Ancre; 9. Ancre Valley and Albert Railway; 10. Hamel; 11. Thiepval; 12. Wonder Werk; 13. Leipzig Salient; 14. Blighty Valley; 15. Dugouts at Authuille; 16. Authuille; 17. Authuille Wood; 18. British Front Line (1st July); 19. German Front Line (1st July); 20. Nordwerk; 21. Thiepval Chateau; 22. Quarry; 23. Mouquet Farm.

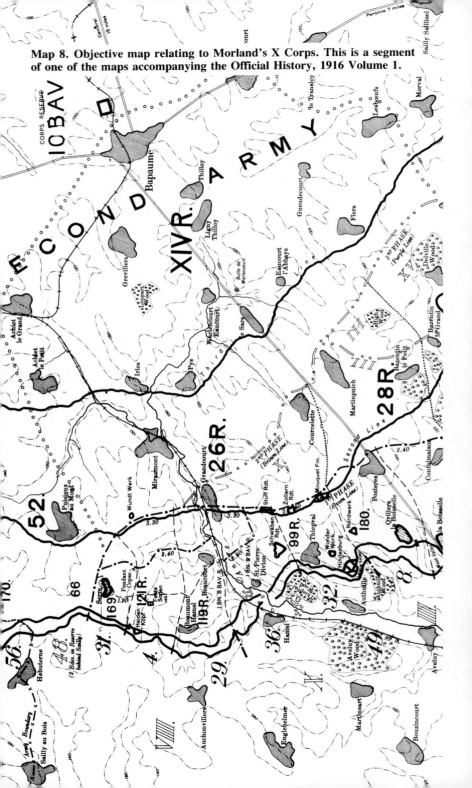

Map 8. Objective map relating to Morland's X Corps. This is a segment of one of the maps accompanying the Official History, 1916 Volume 1.

of Thiepval, by the close of their first day's advance, two hours and forty minutes after zero hour. They were therefore expected to have achieved an advance from their own front lines averaging one and a half miles. It was a fearsome task. The revised plan involved the assault brigades in reaching the Schwaben Redoubt and the intermediate positions of the Hansa Line in the case of the 36th Division, and Thiepval village and the Mouquet Switch Line in the case of the 32nd, before the support brigades took over for the final assault on the relevant parts of the German second line positions. The artillery barrage plans were, therefore, complex. In front of the Ulster Division, for example, after the final intensive bombardment the barrage would lift from the front line onto the 'A.1' lines, and from there onto the 'B' lines three minutes later, at which location the barrage would stay for a further 15 minutes.[3] At 'zero' plus twenty eight minutes the barrage would move to the 'C' lines. At 'zero' plus one hour and eighteen minutes onto the 'D' lines, where the barrage would halt in order to allow the passing forward of 107 Brigade, after which the barrage would lift forward, at zero plus two hours and thirty eight minutes, to a position three hundred yards east of the 'D' lines. The 'D' lines were thus the final objective of the Ulstermen, in their case being the German second position running north from Goat Redoubt, through Stuff Redoubt and on towards Grandcourt. At each lift the 18 pounder and 4.5″ howitzers would search or 'walk' up the communication trenches, either trapping the defenders there or driving them eastwards, away from the assault troops.

The 32nd Division's plans stipulated that the western face of the Leipzig Redoubt would be attacked by two battalions of 97 Brigade, the 16th and 17th Highland Light Infantry. The south face was not to be subjected to an infantry assault. Once the 16th and 17th HLI had taken Leipzig redoubt and moved forward to Mouquet Switch trench the follow up would be undertaken by the men of 14 Brigade, who would pass over the redoubt en route for their later assault on the second line positions around Goat Redoubt.

The bad weather, which at the last moment produced a two day delay in the launch of the Somme offensive from 29th June to 1st July, created both a catastrophe and a noteworthy and optimistic coincidence for the Ulstermen. The catastrophe occurred at Martinsart where, because of the delay, the 13th Royal Irish Rifles were preparing to replace the 11th Battalion in the lines. As the last platoon of C Company was forming up the men were struck by a single shell which killed fourteen and wounded a further forty, of whom seven subsequently died of their wounds. The scene was

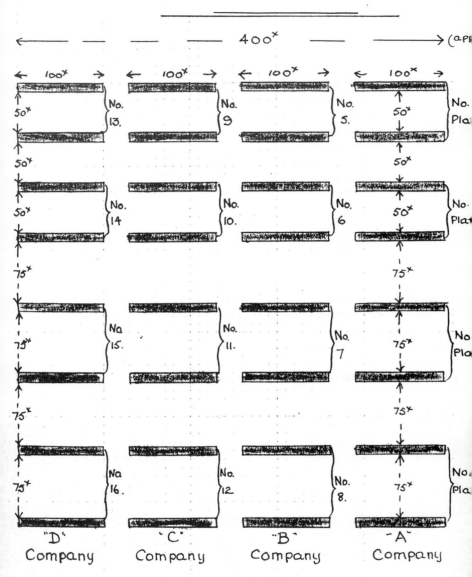

A typical disposition of a single battalion's platoons for the attack on 1st July. This diagram represents one of the Ulster battalions' men as instructed by their divisional command. Source PRO WO95/2491.

one of almost unimaginable horror. Among the wounded were the battalion's second in command and the adjutant. Among the dead were a company sergeant major and the Regimental Sergeant Major.[4] Nevertheless, according to the Julian calendar the 1st July was the anniversary of the Battle of the Boyne in 1690 which saw the victory of William of Orange. As a consequence the Loyalists, especially the three battalions of the Inniskilling Fusiliers,[5] were buoyed up by what was regarded, throughout the division, as a fine and optimistic omen.

The early assaults on 1st July, 1916

I have described these events in a series of snapshots, starting on the German right on the banks of the Ancre near to St. Pierre Divion. The description then moves south-eastwards up the Mill Road and Thiepval Road, thence south past Thiepval and the west face of Leipzig Redoubt. Finally we can travel east along the south face of that salient towards Blighty Valley and the corresponding British salient known as The Nab. One noteworthy fact is that the time for the attack was only notified to many company officers serving with 32nd Division after midnight, and to the men even later, after daybreak. This was an enormous cause of concern since many expected to attack at least under the cover of the half-light of early dawn. By 7.30 am, zero, the sky was a deep blue and the last vestiges of mist had already withered.

Cavalry wait in anticipation of a breakthrough on the morning of 1st July, 1916.

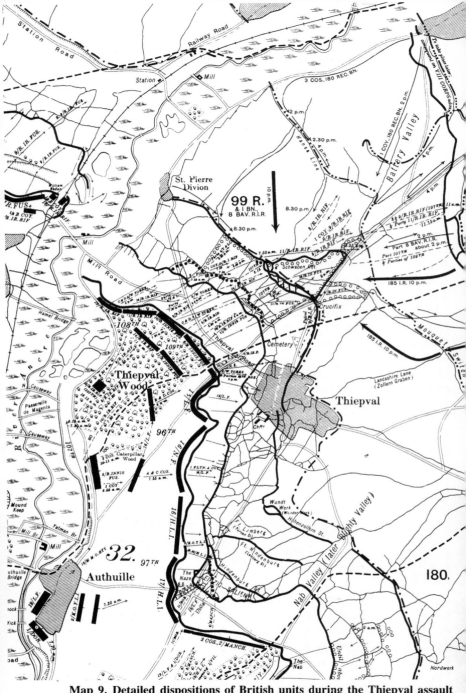

Map 9. Detailed dispositions of British units during the Thiepval assault on 1st July, 1916, Official History map.

1. The assault past St. Pierre Divion by the right half of 108 Brigade

I would suggest that the best vantage point from which to visualize this attack is near to the Ulster Tower.

The Ulstermen's assault in this vicinity was opposed by III Battalion of 99 RIR, commanded by Hauptman Mandel, supported by one company of 8 Bavarian RIR.

The extreme left of the 36th (Ulster) Division attacked north west of the Ancre towards Beaucourt, north of St. Pierre Divion. This attack was made by two battalions of 108 Brigade, the 12th Royal Irish Rifles and the 9th Royal Irish Fusiliers, and they were repulsed.[6] As a direct consequence the German machine guns in Beaucourt Redoubt, confident that they were not under immediate threat on their front, quickly enfiladed the first advance of the 13th (1st County Down Volunteers) and 11th (South Antrim Volunteers) Royal Irish Rifles south east of the mill on the Ancre. It is worth giving re-emphasis to the fact that the plan of attack detailed in the 36th Division's records clearly states that there was to be no assault on St. Pierre Divion during the first minutes of their advance. Fortunately the first moves of the 36th Division, as they debouched from Thiepval Wood into No Man's Land, were hidden from Thiepval's defenders by a smoke screen thrown into the re-entrant north-east of Hammerhead Sap between Thiepval and Schwaben. The men were also greatly advantaged by the artillery preparation which had been enormously thorough here. 'Practically the whole of the wire was destroyed and the [German] trenches so smashed that men who had previously entered them on raiding expeditions did not recognize them.'[7]

The 11th Royal Irish Rifles' men aimed to cross the German front lines between points A18 and A15, a stretch of trench running from the Ulster Tower to a position three hundred yards east. However, on the left of the 11th Battalion the intense fire coming from Beaucourt Redoubt pushed the men of 13th Royal Irish Rifles rather to their right and further up the slopes towards Schwaben Redoubt than was intended. That enfilade fire from Beaucourt became even more intense as machine guns in St. Pierre Divion were brought up from their deep shelters and virtually wiped out any remaining men of the 13th Royal Irish Rifles caught in the open. This was unfortunate in that it left the enemy in the Steinweg trench, which ran back towards Grandcourt, unopposed and the German artillery units in Battery Valley un-threatened. The survivors of the 13th Battalion's initial assault soon found themselves pinned down in the first two lines of German forward trenches around Q.24.d.9.7 where bombing blocks were erected to secure the left flank of the Ulsters' advance. All the battalion's company officers had become casualties and only two platoons had pressed forward to the B lines. It was to this position that Captain Davidson of the 108th Machine Gun Company was sent with two reserve machine guns. Today this scene can be located one hundred and fifty yards north-west of the Ulster Tower, on the far side of the St. Pierre Divion road. Meanwhile the 11th Royal Irish Rifles traversed Mill Road across a No Mans Land which was more than three hundred and fifty yards wide here, having debouched from the very northern tip of Thiepval Wood. They passed the front German fire trench without real casualties. The 11th Royal Irish Rifle's diary recorded at 7.50 am that 'nothing was seen of the 13th R. Ir. Rif on our left either at this or any other time during the battle and in consequence our left flank was always unprotected.' However, since they were further away from the German machine guns firing from the north, the 11th Royal Irish Rifles were able to make better progress. By 8.15 these men were consolidating the forward face of Schwaben Redoubt (or the 'Parallelogram' as it was known to the Ulstermen) at 'Clones', later moving across the Hansa Line to take up a position north-east of Schwaben around points 'Omagh' and 'Strabane', by 9.00 am.

One of the German machine gun teams similar to those operating in the vicinity of Thiepval during the summer of 1916. *Whitehead*

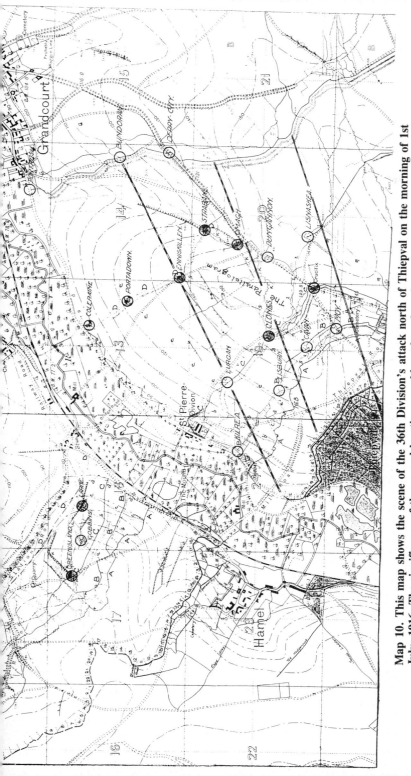

Map 10. This map shows the scene of the 36th Division's attack north of Thiepval on the morning of 1st July, 1916. The significance of the named locations would not have been lost on the men from Belfast and its surrounding area. The name 'Parallelogram' was commonly used in 36th Division literature to denote Schwaben Redoubt.

A similar story unfolded around the use of the support battalion here, the 15th Royal Irish Rifles which was attached to 108 Brigade. Their two left hand support companies' experience mirrored that of the 13th Battalion. On the right the companies made better progress and many men advanced past the B lines. 9.00 am however marked the end of the period within which the 11th Royal Irish Rifles, and the two right support companies of the 15th, suffered few casualties. From now on they would be under heavy machine gun fire from both flanks throughout the day. However, further to their right the men of 109 Brigade had been even more successful.

2. The assault across Thiepval Road by 109 Brigade

The events outlined here can best be visualized from the track on the west of the communal cemetery, four hundred metres north of Thiepval on the D151.

109 Brigade's objectives included the Schwaben Redoubt and the Mouquet Switch Lines to the immediate east of the Schwaben Redoubt. The redoubt was garrisoned by 11 Coy 99 RIR and 4 Coy 8 Bavarian RIR. As with all the 36th Division's attacks at 7.30 this morning, the 9th and 10th Royal Inniskilling Fusiliers had crept out across the sunken road towards what little was left of the German wire. Such was the concentration of the smoke, artillery and trench mortar barrage that they were also able to do this in broad daylight just minutes before the assault began. The 10th 'Skins' report on these operations mentions that at:

'7.15 am on a beautiful summer morning the two leading companies began to issue by platoons through the [prepared] gaps in our wire into No Man's Land and form into extended line with about three paces interval and in this formation crept cautiously up till the leading line was within 100 yards of the German 'A' line where it lay down to wait the signal for assault.'

At that signal the speed of their advance upon the German first line was so rapid that few, if any, German machine guns in front of Schwaben were brought into action against them. Hardly a man in the 10th Skins was seen to fall at this early stage as the lines advanced across the tall summer grasses of No Man's Land. The 9th Skins, to the right of the 10th Battalion, suffered more casualties from the enfilade fire of at least one machine gun in Thiepval Fort which was already trained on the Ulstermen passing north of the village.

However, the German front and immediate support trenches

were simply overrun by the Ulstermen from Derry and Tyrone and they drove forward towards the Schwaben Redoubt. As they moved forward all of these men came within range of the Thiepval machine gun teams who had effectively repulsed the attacks of the 15th Lancashire Fusiliers (1st Salford Pals) and the 16th Northumberland Fusiliers on the trenches west and south-west of Thiepval itself. As the Derry and Tyrone men crossed the skyline their right hand unit, the 9th Royal Inniskilling Fusiliers, suffered increasingly heavy casualties from this enfilade fire. Behind them the men of the 11th Inniskillings and 14th Royal Irish Rifles suffered terrible casualties as they emerged from Thiepval Wood in support of the 9th and 10th Inniskillings. By now the German machine gun at Thiepval cemetery was in action since the British barrage had lifted past the 'B' lines. The last remnants of the British smoke screen had cleared and visibility in front of Thiepval was good. It was apparent that the great bowl of land bisected by Thiepval Road was now bloodied by the 'ghastly spectacle' of hundreds of dead and dying soldiers. However, by 8.00 am, the front face of Schwaben, the German reserve line, was secured by 109 Brigade's assault battalions and half an hour later these indefatigable soldiers were through Schwaben and onto the Mouquet Switch lines, having sent back hundreds of prisoners, many of whom were glad of the chance to outpace their escorts across the terrors of the battlefield and back into Thiepval Wood!

In the heat of the battle these German prisoners stood little chance. Again, the 10th Skins report was graphic in its description of what happened to the first clutches of captured men:

'Enemy prisoners now began to come in, most of them having evidently been concealed in deep dug-outs in the German support trench which runs close behind their front trench. They seemed for the most part dazed and bewildered by the fury of our bombardment and were only too glad to surrender and throw down their arms. They were sent back under escort to our trenches — about sixteen prisoners to each escorting soldier. The first batches of these prisoners were so anxious to reach the shelter of our trenches that they outstripped their escort in the dash across the open and meeting our reinforcing lines coming forward were bayonetted by them in the heat of the moment. Some reached our trenches and were there hunted by the few of our men remaining in our front line...'

This was almost predictable since the 'reinforcing lines' were one of those support battalions, the 11th Royal Inniskilling Fusiliers, who had already suffered heavy casualties from the machine guns in Schwaben and Thiepval which now had the range of the Ulster units crossing No Man's Land. Although the 9th Skins were terribly thinned in numbers they had managed to take their objective, point C8 'Lisnaskea' (R.20.c.7.4) on the Mouquet Switch, three hundred metres east of Schwaben, where a 'mere handful of men under 2 Lieut McKinley held on...'

3. The further advance of 107 Brigade

The terrain here is dominated by the Schwaben Redoubt. For a fine all round view of the area seek the high ground just east of la Grande Ferme.

107 Brigade's attack was marked by incredible bravery and misfortune. Their objective was the 'D' line near Stuff Redoubt and then to work northwards towards the Ancre along the D lines, that is the main German 2nd position. At 5.00 am, the 8th, 9th and 10th Royal Irish Rifles of 107 Brigade had left their assembly trenches in Aveluy, just north west of Lancashire Dump, and marched across the Ancre to Speyside where they lay down to await orders. For these men of 107 Brigade zero, at 7.30 am, meant they would move up through Thiepval Wood, past Gordon Castle and Ross Castle. On that morning of 1st July, 1916, just minutes into their attack the 36th Division's assault battalions were already far too exposed in their own self made salient. Consequently the advance of 107 Brigade, through Thiepval Wood, would inevitably be observed from Thiepval which was still securely held by the Germans. 107 Brigade's Ulstermen would therefore be exposed to a torrent of machine gun fire before they even approached the British front line. The CO of the 9th Royal Irish Rifles, Lieutenant Colonel Percy Crozier, caught a snapshot of these events in his mind:

> 'As we pass Gordon Castle we pick up coils of wire and iron posts. I feel sure in my innermost thoughts these things will never be carried all the way to the final objective; however, even if they get half way it will be a help. Then I glance to the right through a gap in the trees. I see the 10th Rifles plodding on and then my eyes are riveted on a sight I shall never see again. It is the 32nd Division at its best. I see rows upon rows of British soldiers lying dead, dying or wounded in no man's land.'

These were the Tyneside Commercials and Salford Pals whose attacks had already been broken below Thiepval. Crozier well knew what that catastrophe meant for him and his men. The 10th Royal Irish Rifles on Crozier's right were especially exposed through the thin veil of shattered trees and their commanding officer, Colonel Bernard, became one of the many killed whilst passing Ross Castle that morning. On exiting from Elgin Avenue one of the most memorable lines was uttered by Major George Gaffikin as he passed his CO 'Good-bye, Sir, good luck,' he shouted, *en passant*, 'tell them I died a teetotaller, put it on the stone if you find me.'[8]

107 Brigade's men who survived the carnage within Thiepval Wood had then crossed No Man's Land and passed through the forward units of 108 and 109 Brigades at Mouquet Switch and the Hansa Line by 9.15 am. By this time the two German machine guns near Thiepval Chateau were causing many casualties amongst 107 Brigade's men. Simultaneously X Corps had issued orders to withhold the final advance of 107 Brigade but it proved impossible, by any means, to inform the forward units. Forty-five minutes later their leading waves were within one hundred yards of the main German second line defences on the Mouquet Farm − Grandcourt line and seemed likely to be able to sweep in virtually unopposed. Tragically, here, the men ran into the British barrage which was not timed to lift forward and past the Grandcourt, 'D', line until 10.10 am. By the time that lift came the German defences had reorganized and as the Ulstermen stood up again and moved forward they were hit in enfilade by machine gun fire from Grandcourt, from the direction of St. Pierre Divion and from across the Ancre from within the Beaucourt Redoubt. One Brigade diary later commented wryly that, 'if it had not been for [the] barrage we could have taken D line sitting. The wire was sufficiently cut.'[9] Two small groups did, however, get into the Grandcourt lines. About fifty men entered the Stuff Redoubt, and found it unoccupied. A second group fought their way into the trenches three hundred yards further north towards Grandcourt. Two hundred men reached the upper part of Battery Valley but the remainder of 107 Brigade and the remnants of 109 and 108 Brigades who had been swept forward with them were now pinned down in exposed grassland in front of the German second line positions. The Ulsters' position was summed up at 10.20 am by Captain James Davidson of 108 Brigade's Machine Gun Company, who was holding the left of the Ulsters' advance:

> 'Am in B line and have got up two Vickers guns, am consolidating both. Cannot say how many infantry are in line, but in this part there are only about 30 men of the 13th, 11th

and 15th Royal Irish Rifles. We cannot possibly advance and reinforcements, ammunition and bombs most urgently needed.'[10]

By 11.00 am the small numbers of the 36th Division's troops in the D lines began to fall back to the C lines (Hansa lines) where they joined with the men already there in attempts at scraping shelter and consolidating their gains.

Had it been possible to establish a stable line from Mill Road, across the summit of Schwaben Redoubt and on to Stuff Redoubt, and to reinforce those positions with fresh men, ammunition and trench mortars, and to protect them with a barrage capable of preventing German counter attacks, then Thiepval village and the ridge behind would have become vulnerable. In the circumstances reinforcement across the No Mans Land, bisected by the Thiepval Road north-west of that village, became impossible as machine gun fire swept the area without remission. The terrible dilemma in which the Ulstermen found themselves was due to two inescapable facts. On their right the Salford Pals and the Tyneside Commercials' attacks on the village of Thiepval had failed and on their left the 29th Division's attacks towards Beaumont Hamel had also come to naught.

Much was written during the twenties and thirties about these failures.[11] The perspective of those historians who enthused about the Ulster's success suggested that if only the 32nd Division had acquitted itself better the Ulstermen's advance could have provided the stepping stone for success all along the Thiepval plateau and, therefore, via the observation which Schwaben afforded, northwards in the direction of Redan Ridge and Serre. In reality the Salford, Newcastle and Glasgow battalions did all that could have been asked of them. Even the normally understated Official History, accustomed to dealing with failure in its account of the opening of the Battle of the Somme, was moved to say that, 'only bullet proof soldiers could have taken Thiepval on this day'.

4. The Pals' attacks on Thiepval

The best location to envisage these events is from behind the 15th Lancashire Fusiliers' lines on the east face of Thiepval Wood. In front of you the land dips down 200 yards to the Salford Pals' front lines. On your right is Caterpillar Copse, 300 yards east of which stood the Tyneside Commercials' front lines which were on the right of the Salfords. On your left the north-eastern corner of Thiepval Wood marked the boundary between the 36th and 32nd Division's attacks on the morning of 1st July.

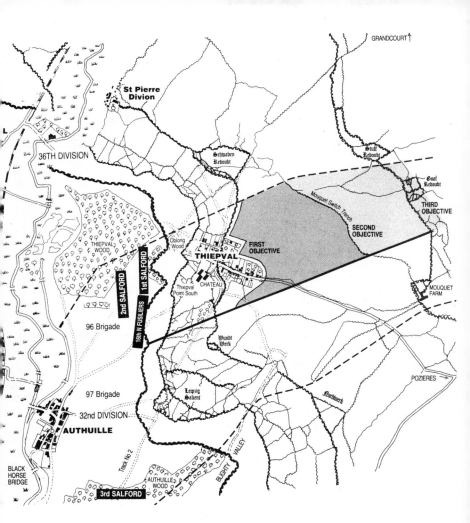

Map 11. This map shows the scene of the Pals' attacks in front of Thiepval on the morning of 1st July, 1916.

The 15th Lancashire Fusiliers (1st Salford Pals) attacked the village of Thiepval directly. Their cause was hopeless in the face of uncut wire and overwhelmingly heavy machine gun and rifle fire. The German unit within Thiepval was II Battalion 99 RIR, commanded by Major Sauer, and their unit history[12] talks of their men's 'indescribable battle joy' as 'our garrison finished wave on wave of the attackers'. Around the barbed wire in front of the village some hand to hand fighting ensued and many of the disorientated Pals were forced to crawl back towards their own

TO THE GLORY OF GOD
AND IN AFFECTIONATE REMEMBRANCE
OF
EDGAR HAMPSON,
LIEUTENANT, 15TH LANCASHIRE FUSILIERS
A SUNDAY SCHOOL TEACHER OF THIS PARISH,
WHO FELL IN ACTION AT THIEPVAL, FRANCE
JULY 1ST, 1916,
ÆTÄTIS 20 YEARS.

THIS TABLET WAS ERECTED BY HIS PARENTS.

Just one of the many personal memorials which were established to commemorate the men who fell in front of Thiepval. In this case Edgar Hampson, son of a Salford newspaper proprietor, who was one of twenty-one officer casualties and 449 casualties amongst the 'other ranks' of the 15th Lancashire Fusiliers, the 1st Salford Pals (out of twenty-four officers and 650 other ranks who made the attack that day). The memorial stands in Lower Broughton church, Salford.

lines. Some small parties of the Salford men penetrated the German first line after which contact with them was lost.[13] One unfortunate consequence was that X Corps then concluded that Thiepval was held, in part at least, by British troops. The village itself was therefore not subjected to artillery fire throughout the rest of the day. The 16th Northumberland Fusiliers (the Tyneside Commercials) were shot down before they were able to reach their opponent's first line of trenches. Their battalion war diary was bitter in its condemnation of the treatment the men had received at the hands of their executioners:

'When the barrage lifted A and B Coys moved forward in waves and were instantly fired upon by Enemy's MG and snipers. The enemy stood upon their parapet and waved to our men to come on and picked them off with rifle fire. The Enemy's fire was so intense that the advance was checked and the waves, or what was left of them, were forced to lie down. On observing this, C Coy, the support Coy, moved out to reinforce the front line, losing a great number of men in doing so ... orders were given for D Coy, the reserve Coy, to advance. Getting over the parapet the first Platoon lost a great number of men and the remainder of the Coy was ordered to "stand fast" and hold the line.'

Throughout the day the German artillery fired on No Man's Land here. Of the British artillery fire on Thiepval's front lines it was said 'only very occasionally that it appeared to be heavy and effective.' The German machine gunners and rifle men were able to pour aimed fire into any movement out in No Man's Land throughout the day, here in front of Thiepval.

5. The remaining 7.30 am attacks on the Thiepval Spur

To visualize these events properly it is necessary to position yourself within the tip of the Leipzig Salient. This can be easily accomplished by strolling past the Memorial to the Missing in Thiepval and along the gravel path which leads south-west in the direction of Aveluy Wood. As you leave the memorial grounds continue straight ahead along the farm track towards the stand of trees six hundred metres distant. Here, south of Thiepval village, one further momentous success was achieved. This was the storming of the Granatloch by the 17th Highland Light Infantry (HLI). The troops garrisoning this area were I Battalion 99 RIR, commanded by Major Baron von Merscheidt-Hullessem.

One of the best known of all overly optimistic assessments had been made before the attack by the 16th and 17th HLI. Their Brigadier enthused that, 'from what is known, I am convinced that the German lines are full of men, but they will be in their dugouts. This being the case, 'Tread closely on the heels of our barrage' should be the motto. I feel sure that the wire generally has been well cut...'[14]

Like so many of the Ulstermen the 17th HLI had crept forward, under cover of the final 'hurricane' bombardment, in their case to within thirty or forty yards of the German positions. As the barrage had lifted they were able to rush forward across adequately cut wire and take the tip of the salient before the German troops found time to clamber up their dugouts' steps. Having taken the redoubt these men then stormed on across the open towards the Hindenburg

Map 12. This map shows locations above Authuille Wood, the scene of the abortive attacks upon the Granatloch early on 1st July, 1916. Trench map Ovillers, 57.d.S.E.4.

Stellung, before which many fell in a vain attempt to capture that position. On their left their sister battalion the 16th HLI, whose initial objective was to overrun the *Wundt-Werk* , found the first lines of wire entanglements intact and the machine gun fire impenetrable. Their casualties were nineteen officers and 492 other ranks in making almost no progress apart from small groups on the right of their attack, under the command of Lieutenant McClaren, who were able to join the 17th's men. Nevertheless, the 17th HLI with support from the 2nd KOYLI, and later from men who survived the subsequent and disastrous 14 Brigade attack, were able to secure their hold on the quarry. The ability of these men to hold this position was greatly assisted by the existence of a covered sap, Sanda Sap, which had been dug beneath No Mans Land and now connected the old British front line with the newly captured Granatloch. This success proved to be the most northerly permanent 'bite' into the German positions during 1st July.

Catastrophically though, the success at Granatloch led to further and enormous waste of life. The 17th HLI and 2nd KOYLI attempted further progress towards the rear of the Leipzig Salient, both by advance across the open and by using bombing parties to bomb around the flanks. All such attempts were repelled by the intensity of machine gun fire from the unmolested *Wundt-Werk* and the stubbornness of the German resistance. At 8.30 am the 11th Borders (the Lonsdales), who were the reserve for the 97 Brigade, left their positions in Authuille Wood, the men expecting to find Leipzig Salient in British hands. In fact the battalion should never have left the shelter of Authuille Wood since it was already clear, and known to 32nd Division, that the 8th Division on their right had made no inroads into the Nordwerk positions. Nevertheless, the 11th Borders advance was made, along the track running towards Thiepval from the direction of Aveluy through Authuille Wood and which enters the tip of the Leipzig Salient at the Granatloch. The Lonsdales were shot down in droves by enfilade machine gun fire from the Nordwerk as they moved towards what should have been their jumping off trenches. Having witnessed this catastrophe Colonel Machell struggled forward to reach the remnants of his beloved men in the British front line. Without hesitation Machell led them over the top only to be shot down instantly. A few men on the left of the battalion succeeded in gaining the sanctuary of the quarry opposite. Although this battalion's experience is often cited as one of the worst exemplars of severe casualties on 1st July, the majority of its casualties were wounded since shellfire was negligible and rifle fire too high. (ORs:

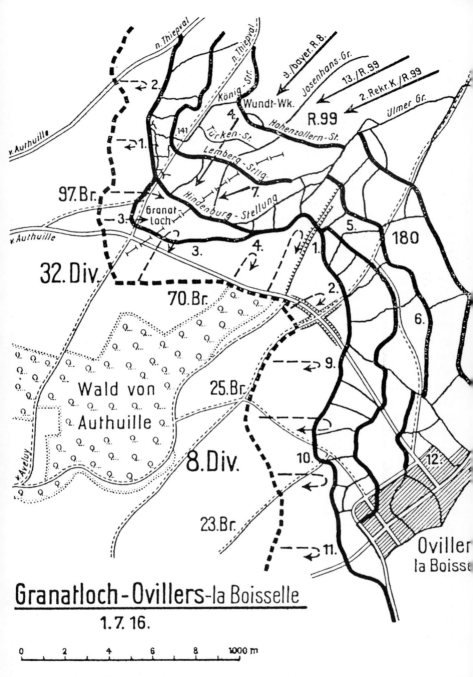

Map 13. The fighting in the Granatloch positions showing the German reinforcements and their movements during the day.

100 killed, nineteen missing and 371 wounded. Officers: eleven killed or DoW, fourteen wounded.) Five days later the battalion diary records its strength as 'eleven officers & 480 O.R.'.

6. The disastrous attacks by 14 Brigade

Today the location of the following actions correspond to a point due south of the crossroads just below the quarry or Granatloch along to a position in the hollow of Blighty Valley as it leaves Authuille Wood six hundred metres south-east of the quarry crossroads on the Ovillers road. This road is therefore a good location to visualize these attacks from.

Perhaps nothing in the long history of the British Army's battles at Thiepval could match the dreadful farrago which subsequently unfolded across the terrain now littered with the bodies of the Lonsdales. This was a classical example of the chaos and indecision which the circumstance of battle can bring about when communication is indirect or broken.

The forward movement of troops had now taken on an inexorable and self perpetuating inevitability. The reserve brigade for the 32nd Division was 14 Brigade and their task was to pass through the Leipzig Salient where they were to assault the German second line positions beyond Mouquet Farm, in the vicinity of Goat Redoubt. Simultaneously, it was hoped, the 36th Division's reserve brigade, the 107th, would be assaulting Stuff Redoubt five hundred metres north of Goat. It had been presumed, perhaps wrongly, that it would not be appropriate to assault the south face of the Leipzig positions. This was because of the presumption that the HLI's attacks would have swept across the south of the redoubt from the west in an easterly direction and that any simultaneous assault from the south would have confused and overcomplicated the attack. Therefore there was no attack launched from the British trenches running from Chequerbent Street past Boggart Hole Clough to Mersey Street (X.1.a.1.5 to X.1.b.3.3).

14 Brigade was divided into two columns. Soon after 7.00 am the 1st Dorsets had left Black Horse shelters, closely followed by the 19th Lancashire Fusiliers. The Dorsets were to lead the advance of the left column. It was reported that as they marched forward:

'A battery of artillery was in action half way in [Authuille] wood, enemy sending heavy shrapnel all over the place searching for us. (Naturally we got the thickest time, as 97 Brigade had already debouched from the front of the wood, and the enemy guessed more to follow.) We had a number of casualties there, and passed by a number of killed and wounded from our leading companies. We had a terrible dose of machine gun fire sweeping us through the wood, could not understand why. If front and second line had been carried, enemy machine guns would be out of action.'[15]

At 8.45 the battalion left the relative security of Authuille wood, seemingly intent on self destruction having witnessed the destruction of the men from Cumberland and Westmoreland. With massive understatement the Dorset's diary recorded that, 'it was apparent that matters were not progressing quite as favourably as had been anticipated.' In an exact replica of the Lonsdale's attack the Dorsets were also decimated, their diary noting that, 'the end of DUMBARTON TRACK and the ground up to our front line trench was covered with our killed and wounded; yet the men continued to jump up and advance over their fallen comrades as the word to go was given.'

A handful of their officers and sixty men made it into Leipzig. The Dorsets were followed into this cauldron by the 19th Lancashire Fusiliers, the 3rd Salford Pals. The Fusilier's Commanding Officer, Lieutenant-Colonel Graham, made every effort to disguise their attack by ordering a smoke screen to their right, fired by the Brigade trench mortars. It proved to have some benefit in reducing casualties although, in most other respects, the outcome of the Salford's attack was the same as that effected by the Lonsdales and Dorsets. Fewer than fifty of the Fusiliers gained the relative safety of the redoubt opposite and the battalion 'experienced two hundred and sixty eight casualties − that is to say 50% of its fighting strength − having twenty officers and 577 other ranks when going into action'. These events gave the 32nd Division's commanding Officer, Major General W.H. Rycroft, the chance to record his opinion that 'The 19th Lancashire Fusiliers seemingly did not leave our trenches'![16]

It was apparent that the slaughter was being orchestrated from the *Nordwerk* and in an act of mercy the right hand column, consisting of men belonging to the 15th HLI and the 2nd Manchesters, were ordered to stand fast. Later in the day, at 1.45 pm, two platoons of the 2nd Manchesters also managed to enter the Naze/Granatloch lodgement to reinforce the exhausted troops already there. The Manchesters found the 'trenches at the NAZE were packed with 17th HLI, 2nd KOYLI, 1st Dorsets and 11th Borders and 19th LF. Only four officers were present and the whole were in a state of complete demoralisation.' It was not surprising. For six hours these men had been progressively whittled

German artillerymen pose with their guns on the Somme, 1916.

away under a devastating artillery, machine gun and grenade barrage. By 6.00 pm the rest of the 2nd Manchesters took over the redoubt by keeping to the far left and using Rock Street and Sanda Street before advancing across the open at the Naze, thereby escaping the enfilade from the Nordwerk. Later in the evening Sanda Sap was opened but not for the safe travel of German prisoners. Such was the ill feeling that the 2nd Manchesters diary records in brutal terms that, 'Considerable enjoyment was given to our troops by Lieutenant Robertson who made the prisoners run across the open through their own Artillery Barrage, upon reaching our line these men were kept out of our dugouts by the sharp end of a bayonet.'[17] Such was the disregard for the conventions relating to the fair treatment of prisoners by their captors. In the heat of battle such attitudes are understandable.

7. German Counter Attacks and the Retirement of the Ulster Division

These events are best understood from the German perspective, so try a position to the rear of Stuff Redoubt (R.21 central) at the top of Stump Road, and then walk onto the higher ground of the Schwaben Redoubt (R.20.a.0.0). It is worth saying here that this section of the countryside around Thiepval is almost featureless and a map and compass would certainly help give your walk meaning.

As the morning of 1st July wore on the exposure of the Ulsters became complete. Their positions were assailed by all arms fire, their supply of ammunition almost gone, their route to the rear cut off. By 12.40 pm Captain Davidson's Vickers guns had been lost and he had been forced to fall back. He reported, 'I am holding the end of a communication trench in A line with a few bombers and a Lewis Gun. We cannot hold much longer. We are being pressed on all sides and ammunition is almost finished.' By 12.50 Colonel Savage, commanding the 13th Royal Irish Rifles, was desperate in his desire to reinforce his men holding the left of the Ulsters' advance. 'I then sent up the few remaining batt'n staff, the orderly room Sergt, 2 officer's servants, 2 Coy QM Sergts with ammunition, these men were unable to cross No Man's Land. Two were killed, three wounded.'[18] Everywhere behind the Ulsters' advance the position was the same, no reinforcements or ammunition could be got across the fire swept zone. Nevertheless, later in the afternoon a patrol was sent towards Thiepval from the Crucifix at point B13 on the south of Schwaben Redoubt but were driven away. Another patrol managed to travel to within five hundred yards of Mouquet Farm, along the Switch Line. The penetration of the Thiepval positions by this gallant band revealed the one remaining weakness in the German position. It can only remain a matter of conjecture as to what would have occurred if reserves had been available to pour down the Switch and take Thiepval in reverse.

Since mid-day the Ulstermen attempting to consolidate within Schwaben Redoubt had been shelled heavily by German artillery units. This was the cover for a two pronged assault on the advanced positions of the Ulstermen. The first of these was the attack of the 180th Regiment's recruit battalion who moved up from Grandcourt, forcing the withdrawal of the forward Ulstermen in Battery Valley. Some of these young German drafts then bombed further up the Hansa lines, to within six hundred yards of the Schwaben Redoubt where their advance was repulsed. Unfortunately that repulse revealed the exact positions occupied by the Royal Irish Rifles and thereafter these men were subjected to prolonged and even more accurate shelling. The other arm of this counter attack developed at 2.00 pm, from Goat Redoubt (*Feste Zollern*) and the trench which connected it with Thiepval, Lancashire Lane or *Zollern Graben*, as well as through Stuff Redoubt. Simultaneously a heavy bombardment with shrapnel and high explosive was opened on the

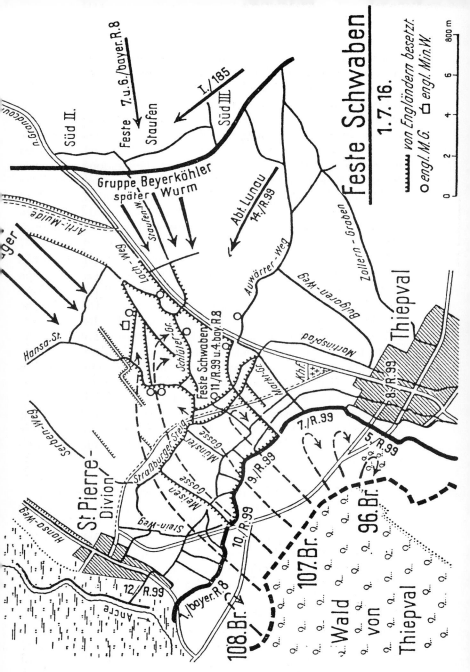

Map 14. This shows the German counter attacks which developed around the Ulstermen in the Schwaben redoubt during the afternoon and early evening of 1st July.

Ulstermen in the A and B lines as well as No Man's Land and the British trenches. The German counter attack then came forward in waves, made up of various companies detached from the 8th Bavarian Reserve Regiment, who gradually pressed towards Schwaben under the cover of the bombardment which was now raining unremittingly onto that position. On each occasion they were repulsed by the dwindling parties of soldiers who survived in that inferno, particularly brave work being done by Lance Corporal Fisher of 109 Brigade's Machine Gun Company. The nearby infantry later reported him, 'to have accounted for several hundreds'! Captain Davidson survived until wounded in the knee in mid afternoon. Returning across the sunken part of Thiepval Road he was shot dead whilst being carried by two comrades.[19]

By late afternoon however it was clear that Feste Schwaben was surrounded on its north, east and south sides. Some Ulstermen still remained within the 'C' lines. Major Peacocke, who was second in command of the 9th Inniskilling Fusiliers, reported from the crucifix near the junction of Mouquet Switch with Schwaben, 'that it might be possible to hold on if bombs, ammunition belts and water for Vickers Guns could be brought up.'[20] As we have seen, that hope was an impossible one and the few remaining parties were becoming dangerously isolated and so exhausted that the men were barely able to move or muster sufficient enthusiasm to save themselves. Indeed 107 Brigade's diary records that, 'Copy of order issued by O.C. 9th R.I.R. that no troops are to retire from C line. C.O. 9th R.I.R. reports that 70 men 108 Bde who were retiring had been sent back and that Lt Finlay had to fire on them.'

Throughout the afternoon pressure mounted on the 49th Division to at least do something to help the beleaguered Ulstermen. At 4.20 146 Brigade was placed at the disposal of 107 Brigade but this still brought little evidence of enthusiasm among Major General Perceval's West Yorkshire territorials for the task in hand. Repeated orders finally brought the necessary action although the hour was now past 7.00 pm, and no Yorkshiremen were able to influence the fight to hold on to Schwaben and the surrounding positions.

It was therefore only a matter of time before the inevitable happened. At 10.00 pm German infantry attacked from all sides. The order to withdraw was given by the two remaining senior officers in the 'Schwaben Parallelogram', Major Peacocke and Captain Montgomery, and the remaining Ulstermen retired to the German front lines, the 'A' line where some men belonging to the 49th Division were found to be in possession.[21] This therefore left the Leipzig Redoubt as the only tangible gain in the Thiepval sector attacked by X Corps. The 2nd Manchesters and 2nd KOYLI had taken over that gain, the 16th and 17th HLI being withdrawn. Further north the 2nd Inniskillings and 16th Lancashire Fusiliers (2nd Salford Pals) garrisoned the front lines opposite Thiepval.

The German machine gun teams in the Thiepval defences had done their work well. Twenty one of the guns survived the day's fighting. Twenty of the guns fired an average of between 8 and 10,000 rounds whilst team 9, firing from the Brauner Weg just south of Thiepval opposite the Tyneside Commercial's attack, fired 18,000 rounds during the defence of Thiepval on 1st July. Each officer and man of the 99 RIR was later estimated to have fired 350 rounds this day. The casualty list amongst the Ulster Division's troops was enormous, 216 officers and 5,266 men;[22] almost 4,000 amongst the 32nd Division's men; under 600 amongst the 49th Division. As twilight deepened those British soldiers who had been pinned down throughout the daylight hours and the walking and crawling wounded struggled back as best they could. Those whose eyes searched the enveloping darkness from the front lines heard no silence, just the sounds of anguished and frightened men in pain, in No Man's Land.

1. 32nd Division.
   14 Brigade.
   19th Lancashire Fusiliers. (3rd Salford Pals)
   1st Dorsetshires.
   2nd Manchesters.
   15th Highland Light Infantry. (Glasgow Tramways)
   96 Brigade.
   16th Northumberland Fusiliers. (Tyneside Commercials)
   15th Lancashire Fusiliers. (1st Salford Pals)
   16th Lancashire Fusiliers. (2nd Salford Pals)
   2nd Royal Inniskilling Fusiliers.
   97 Brigade.
   11th Borders. (The Lonsdales)
   2nd King's Own Yorkshire Light Infantry.
   16th Highland Light Infantry. (Glasgow Boy's Brigade)
   17th Highland Light Infantry. (Glasgow Chamber of Commerce)
   Pioneers.
   17th Northumberland Fusiliers.
   36th Division.
   107 Brigade.
   8th Royal Irish Rifles. (East Belfast Volunteers)
   9th Royal Irish Rifles. (West Belfast Volunteers)
   10th Royal Irish Rifles. (South Belfast Volunteers)
   15th Royal Irish Rifles. (North Belfast Volunteers)

108 Brigade.
11th Royal Irish Rifles. (South Antrim Volunteers)
12th Royal Irish Rifles. (Central Antrim Volunteers)
13th Royal Irish Rifles. (1st County Down Volunteers)
9th Royal Irish Fusiliers. (Armagh, Monaghan and Cavan Volunteers)
109 Brigade.
9th Royal Inniskilling Fusiliers. (Tyrone Volunteers)
10th Royal Inniskilling Fusiliers. (Derry Volunteers)
11th Royal Inniskilling Fusiliers. (Donegal and Fermanagh Volunteers)
14th Royal Irish Rifles. (Young Citizen Volunteers of Belfast)
Pioneers.
16th Royal Irish Rifles. (2nd County Down Volunteers)
49th Division.
146 Brigade.
147 Brigade.
148 Brigade.
2. In view of what subsequently happened on 1st July it is fortunate that Nugent's original plan was not followed since enfilade machine gun fire from the Beaumont-Hamel and Beaucourt areas would have utterly destroyed the Ulstermen before they could have reached Schwaben.
3. The 'A' line was the German front fire trench, 'A1' was the second fire trench, 'B' the third, which also corresponded to the forward face of Schwaben Redoubt. 'C' was the intermediate lines known as Hansa and Mouquet Switch.
4. The men lie in Martinsart British Military Cemetery becoming the first to be buried there. Their graves are in Plot 1, Row A, the first grave being that of Pte William Darragh followed by RSM James Beatson, Rifleman Thomas Bell, Rifleman James Carson, Rifleman Albert Crangle, Rifleman Richard Crawley, Rifleman David Dale, Rifleman Samuel Hamilton, Rifleman George Heenan, Rifleman Alexander Jones, CSM Joseph McCoy, Rifleman Joseph Martin, Rifleman Thomas Mercer and Rifleman Joseph Thompson.
5. Since these battalions had their origins in the men from Enniskillen who took great credit for that victory.

This painting by James Prinsep Beadle, RA, depicts soldiers of the 11th Royal Irish Rifles of 108 Infantry Brigade moving between the A and B lines of German trenches.

6. For example, at the close of the day none of the officers and only 80 of the men from the 9th Royal Irish Fusiliers who had left Elgin Avenue remained unwounded.

7. WO 95/2491.

8. P. Crozier. *A Brass Hat in No Man's Land.*

9. 107 Brigade Diary. WO 95/2502.

10. 13th Royal Irish Rifles' War Diary. WO 95/2506.

11. For example, see *The History of the 36th (Ulster) Division*, Cyril Falls. M'Caw, Stevenson & Orr, Belfast, 1922.

12. *In the Hurricane of the Somme Battle.*

13. See *Salford Pals*, Stedman, Pen & Sword Books Ltd, 1993.

14. Brigadier General J.B.Jardine, DSO, commanding 97th Brigade.

15. Shephard. *A Sergeant-Major's War.*

16. 32nd Division War Diary, Public Record Office, WO95/2368.

17. WO 95/2392.

18. WO 95/2506.

19. He is buried at Serre Road Number 2, the largest British cemetery on the Somme where many remains were concentrated during the 1920s and 30s after being discovered during post war battlefield clearances or subsequent agricultural work.

20. WO 95/2491.

21. The relationship between the 36th and 49th Division was terribly soured by the inability of the Yorkshire Territorials to support and relieve the Ulstermen in their hour of need. The Diary entry made at 11.00 p.m., by the 107th Brigade records that the Brigadier General Commanding 146th Brigade admitted, "Regret to say Batts sent to C8 & C11 have turned back on account of shelling and M.G. fire. Have sent them up again..." Even the reliefs carried out during the subsequent two days were marked by constant confusion, delays and further "misunderstandings".

22. PRO WO95/2491. This figure includes some smaller numbers of casualties incurred on 2nd July as well.

Chapter Four
FURTHER EVENTS ON THIEPVAL RIDGE
DURING THE SUMMER AND AUTUMN OF 1916

On the opening day of the Battle of the Somme the successes of the French Army on the right and the British 30th, 18th and 7th Divisions nearby at Montauban and Mametz changed the focus of the battle. Thiepval now became the fulcrum around which a new emphasis in the fighting swung. During the weeks and months of the Somme offensive which followed the names of Mametz, Trones, Bazentin, Delville and High Woods were carved into history as the emphasis of the fighting developed into an attempt to take advantage of those earliest successes around Montauban and Mametz. Due south of Thiepval the twin villages of Ovillers and La Boisselle, steadfastly defended by the Germans on 1st July, were overcome and intense fighting developed below and eventually around Pozieres. Initially that meant that the footing in the Leipzig salient would have to be enlarged in order to protect the left flank of the progress along the southern part of the Pozieres ridge. Much of that process occurred on 21st August when the south-eastern end of Hindenburg trench and parts of Lemberg trenches were taken. On 24th August the greater part of Hindenburg trench also fell but this marked the end of any British success here during August.

However, the immovable fact remained that Thiepval village had not fallen. Its vicinity still commanded much of the northern end of Pozieres Ridge as well as the ground north of the Ancre from Beaucourt, Beaumont Hamel, past Serre and on towards Gommecourt. Significantly, during the period of July and August, the German defences around Thiepval were strengthened by the deepening and fortification of the communication trenches which ran in an east-west direction both to the north and south of the village. These trenches were to have an immense impact upon the nature of the fighting and it is worth being clear as to exactly where the most important ones were located. In sequence from south to north they were Joseph Trench which ran from the present day entrance to Thiepval Memorial Park eastwards to the Pozieres road; Schwaben Trench which ran along the Pozieres road from the village centre to Mouquet Farm; Zollern Trench (or Lancashire Lane) which ran from Zollern (or Goat) Redoubt into the cottage gardens just east of Thiepval church on the north side of the Pozieres road; Hessian Trench which ran from Stuff Redoubt into the south eastern corner of Schwaben using part of the course of

The dawn sky is illuminated by the flashes of shellfire during the bombardment prior to the assault upon the Thiepval Ridge on 15th September.

the original Mouquet Switch line; and lastly Stuff Trench which left the north-eastern corner of Schwaben in an easterly direction along the heights above the Ancre and Grandcourt.

Ever since the disasters of 1st July it had been obvious that an assault on Thiepval was unavoidable if the Somme offensive was not to be emasculated by the failure to capture any strategically significant location. The eventual taking of Pozieres and the reduction of the Mouquet Farm defences created the opportunity to make that assault on more equal terms than those undertaken during the early hours of 1st July. Between the 15th and 22nd September the Battle of Flers − Courcelette had seen some progress made towards Thiepval. Most notably this had seen some parts of the German defences east and west of the *Wundt-Werk* occupied, as well as an advance towards Mouquet Farm across an utterly-shell torn and devastated landscape.

By the last week in September the German Army had been pushed north of Mouquet Farm and the attack on Thiepval was imminent. Within the confines of our designated area that attack would be undertaken on 26th September by the 11th Division on the right with the 18th Division on their left, both part of II Corps, the command of which was held by Lieutenant General C.W. Jacob who had previously held a command with the Meerut Division. To the right of the 11th Division and outside our area

A long line of British reserve troops standing silhouetted against the skyline at dawn near Thiepval, 15th September.

were the 1st and 2nd Canadian Divisions. The ultimate objective of the 11th and 18th Divisions was Hessian Trench. For the purpose of this attack eight tanks were made available, two to the Canadians and six to the troops attacking Thiepval where the strongest resistance could be anticipated. Such small numbers were an example of what later became known as the 'penny packeting' of tanks, a tactic which tended to diminish their success and breed cynicism in the eyes of infantrymen who regarded the machines as unreliable and likely to draw fire. The real problem, of course, was that so few tanks were available. The steep approaches combined with the confined and trench riddled conditions within Thiepval meant that the location was ill suited to the successful deployment of such ponderous vehicles. Nevertheless, one tank, C5, was instrumental in events here.

In order to introduce and understand the ground to the east of Thiepval it is necessary to travel along the D73 to the Mouquet Farm junction (R.33.a central). This can be reached from either the Thiepval or Pozieres ends of the D73.

During August and September 1916 the Thiepval to Mouquet Farm section of this road had been entrenched and fortified. This was the Schwaben Trench. In front of Schwaben Trench lay Joseph Trench, the new German front line which ran eastwards from the

south of Thiepval village until it joined Schwaben Trench four hundred yards north-west from the Mouquet Farm junction. The lane leading down to Mouquet Farm was the jumping off trench of 34 Brigade, 11th Division, on 26th September. Before the Great War this lane continued past the farm and on into Courcelette. Visitors to the farm will almost certainly see considerable amounts of the debris of war which still accumulates from the fields around here. It is worth noting that the farm today, on the right of the lane, lies on the opposite side of that lane from its pre-war location. Running west from the Mouquet Farm junction, along to the upper reaches of Blighty Valley, was the frontage of 33 Brigade.

Standing on the left of the 11th Divison was the 18th, whose Commander was Ivor Maxse, later to become Inspector General of Training and already a thoroughly experienced and respected leader of men. Throughout a large part of the war this division retained a reputation for innovative tactics, sound staff work, thorough preparation and taking its objectives. Since its involvement in the successful assault on the Pommiers Redoubt positions west of Montauban on 1st July, the division had been to Flanders and had then received three weeks battle training in readiness for its task at Thiepval. The division arrived on 21st September and their forming up trenches had been prepared across

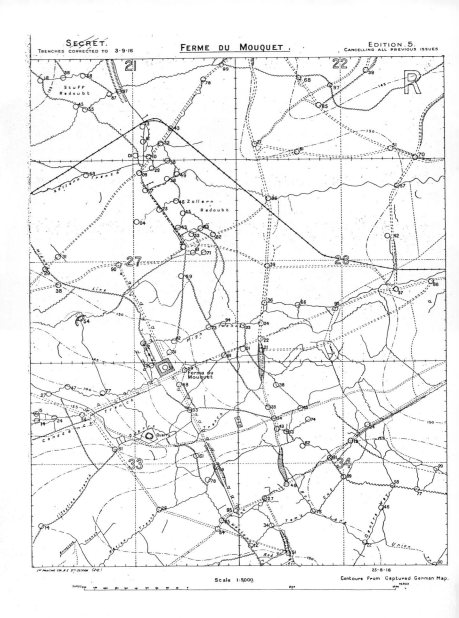

Map 15. The German second position behind Thiepval running from Pozieres, past Mouquet Farm, Goat Redoubt and Stuff Redoubt towards Grandcourt beyond the northern limit of this map.

88

the Authuille spur, above the site of Leipzig Salient. The track running up the spur from the Granatloch to Thiepval formed the junction between 54 Brigade, on the left, and 53 Brigade, on the right. The men's progress to these forming up trenches was protected by two new communication trenches, Pip Street, a newly constructed communication trench which crossed the old No Man's Land south of the original Leipzig Salient, and Prince Street which ran from the Granatloch along the track leading to Thiepval. Further north, across No Man's Land, the German front line known as Joseph Trench ran along its east-west axis just south of the village. Beyond that line the 18th Division would be expected to cross the important support position of Schwaben Trench, running along the Thiepval – Pozieres road. The men's third objective was a portion of Zollern Trench (or Lancashire Lane) and thence westwards along the north-western portion of the village. On the left of the 18th Division 146 Brigade of the 49th Division would hold the original British Front Line, opposite the village, in front of Thiepval Wood. The 18th Division's headquarters for this action was located at Hedauville, west of Martinsart.

The indefatigable Wurtembergers were still the occupants of Thiepval's seemingly impregnable defences and Maxse's plans were dependent upon thorough and complete artillery domination of the field. He was additionally allocated the artillery of the 25th and 49th Divisions as well as a battery of six″ howitzers from II

The lane leading to Mouquet Farm, the jumping off trench of 34 Brigade, 11th Division, at the start of the attacks destined to take Thiepval on 26th September. On the left of the 11th Division were the 18th Division whose name became synonymous with the taking of Thiepval.

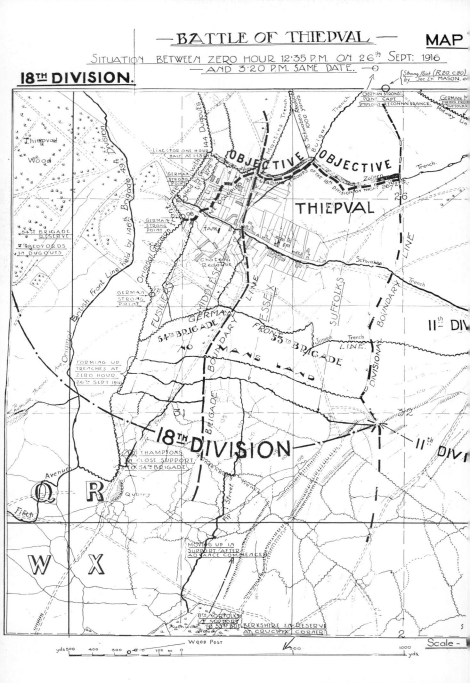

Map 16. The Battle of Thiepval. Part of Ivor Maxse's Map 'X' which details the area surrounding the wreckage of the Chateau.

The view towards the village of Thiepval from the centre of the 18th Division's lines at zero hour, 12.35 pm, on 26th September 1916. To the left of this line 54 Brigade carried the attack deep into Thiepval village. On the right were 5 Brigade who had the 11th division on their right.

Corps. The preliminary bombardment lasted for three days. During that bombardment 60,000 rounds of field artillery shell were fired along with 45,000 rounds of heavier shell. On the afternoon of 24th September Thiepval was also subjected to a heavy gas attack, 500 lachrymatory shells being fired into the village by No.2 Special Company Royal Engineers. The hour set for the final assault was 12.35 pm, 26th September, sensibly chosen in order to allow four hours of autumnal daylight for the success of the assault before the advanced troops began consolidation under the cover of growing darkness and away from observed barrages. The day before the assault every battalion was drilled in the vital importance of Thiepval's observation and the fact that the Germans 'have issued frequent orders to all concerned to hold it "at all costs". They have even boasted in writing that it is impregnable. The 180th Regt. of WURTTENBURGERS [sic] have withstood attacks on THIEPVAL for two years, but the 18th Division will take it tomorrow.'[1]

The 18th Division's operation was a triumph of courage, organization and determination. On their right the 11th Division's men fought equally bravely but the right of that division's attack made slower progress, suffering heavy casualties in the fighting which took them past Mouquet Farm and north towards *Feste Zollern*. However, the left of 11th Division's attack made better progress and some men advanced past Zollern Trench to their ultimate objective of Hessian Trench. On their left the advance of the 8th Suffolks and 10th Essex of 53 Brigade had been notable in that 'from Joseph Trench there suddenly issued a number of Germans running through our barrage towards the advancing Suffolks. They were yelling and shouting and evidently in a state of terror, being half dressed, unarmed, holding their hands high up in the air.' Some other Germans started to follow but then wavered and ran back towards their trench and were shot down. The Suffolk men stuck, with great resolution, to within thirty yards of their own barrage as they passed Schwaben, Zollern and even Bulgar trench in small numbers. The Essex men reached as far forward as Martins Trench but little progress could then be made in the direction of Schwaben Redoubt. In 54 Brigade's area the fighting was even more bloody since the assault covered all of the fortifications in the lines facing Thiepval Wood, assaulted by the 11th Royal Fusiliers, as well as the bulk of the village itself which was attacked by the 12th Middlesex. One of the tanks, HMLS *Creme de Menthe* numbered C5, crossed the No Man's Land from Thiepval Wood and crushed the resistance of the German machine gun teams around Thiepval Chateau before becoming ditched across a trench just yards north of the chateau's ruins. A second tank arrived too late to be of value and was ditched.

The divisional commander's official narrative report portrays exactly how much he thought of the bravery which had achieved the capture of the village fortress of Thiepval:

> '...their achievement will bear comparison with any similar feat of arms in this war. The gallantry displayed by all ranks has been handsomely recognised by the award of numerous decorations and medals to the survivors, but I should be doing an injustice to heroic officers and men and incidentally to the 18th Division if I omitted to record in this official report my opinion of what was accomplished by those who fell in action. They did more than their fair share towards the achievement of the success which the survivors alone celebrate.'[2]

In the face of this assault by the 18th Division the village which had withstood all for two years was taken.

The myth of the Wurtembergers invincibility was broken. By twilight the bulk of the divisional objectives had been occupied and 54 Brigade, whose assault was led by the 11th Royal Fusiliers and the 12th Middlesex, can therefore be credited with the final taking of Thiepval village. The Middlesex men in particular had

HMLS *Creme de Menthe*, C5, ditched just north of Thiepval Chateau having lost part of her rear steering mechanism. The map used by 18th Division during these operations identifies the location at which this tank ground to a halt as R.25.d.3.7. This tank was not recovered and lay there throughout subsequent operations in the area, being used as an oil lamp signalling station and shelter.

The heap of rubble which was once the Chateau at Thiepval.

Aftermath of a British bombardment prior to an attack, German stretcher bearer fatalities in a destroyed section of trench.

Private F.J.Edwards

Private R.Ryder

been encouraged by their Commanding Officer, Lieutenant Colonel Frank Maxwell, VC, to take no prisoners, on the grounds that the enemy should be exterminated and that prisoners only clogged up already congested supply lines. Two members of that Middlesex battalion, Private 2442 Frederick Jeremiah Edwards and Private 3281 Robert Ryder, fought with such gallantry in the events around the heap of rubble marking Thiepval's chateau that they were awarded the Victoria Cross. In both cases their awards resulted from seizing the initiative after all the nearby battalion and company officers had become casualties. In fact the casualties amongst 54 Brigade were extremely heavy and the existence of the 18th Division's memorial at Thiepval is in great measure due to the sacrifice of so many men from the Royal Fusiliers, Middlesex Regiment and their support battalion, the 6th Northamptonshires, who fought so ferociously and willingly here on 26th September, 1916. The CO of the Northamptons, Lieutenant Colonel Ripley, died as a result of wounds received whilst moving forward that day.

Overnight the western flank of the remaining German positions, south of the village's cemetery, were constantly raided and harried by the activities of 146 Brigade operating across No Man's Land. The following morning the remaining north-western portion of Thiepval was taken in a rush by the 7th Bedfordshires, initially 'at the point of the bayonet'. It was during this final act in the clearance of Thiepval that the 22 year old Second-Lieutenant Tom Edwin Adlam would display the conspicuous bravery and gallant leadership which also brought him the Victoria Cross. Adlam's forte was sport, cricket in particular, and his prowess at hurling grenades so demoralized the Germans, who were unable to match his accuracy and length that, when his men's attack was faltering, he was able to re-establish the initiative and drive the remaining

**2nd Lieut
Tom Adlam**

One of the Royal Fusiliers sports a number of trophies taken during the battle for Thiepval village.

An exhausted soldier asleep in a front line trench at Thiepval.

Germans from Thiepval village towards the communal cemetery and Schwaben Redoubt to the north.

The taking of Thiepval cost the 18th Division a total of 1,456 casualties of whom sixty-four were officers. The worst affected battalion was the 12th Middlesex which suffered ten officers and sixty men killed along with eight officers and 233 men wounded. By contrast the Germans had lost enormously more and the loss of this important high ground meant that the tide had now begun to turn in the battle for Thiepval Ridge. The forbidding Schwaben Redoubt now beckoned.

The Capture of Schwaben Redoubt

Whilst the capture of Thiepval had been of great significance, control of the Schwaben Redoubt promised a greater prize. Once this had been achieved it would then be possible to deny the Germans observation over Authuille, Aveluy and on towards Albert, although it is worth saying that very much more restricted view towards Albert could be had from Beaucourt Redoubt. At the same time the British Army would gain observation over the Redan Ridge and north towards Serre and north-east past Grandcourt towards Miraumont. Agonizingly that final half mile would take a further two and a half weeks to achieve completely.

Captain ACT White

Initially the assault was to be made by the 18th Division's 53 Brigade who had experienced less severe casualties in their attacks across the east of the village on 26th September. Meanwhile the 11th Division's troops continued their grim struggle for control of *Feste Staufen* (Stuff Redoubt) and the surrounding areas. In this wilderness of shell-holes and mud Captain Archie White of the Green Howards would win his Victoria Cross whilst leading his men in a valiant attempt to bomb their way into control of Stuff Redoubt's northern face. Although initially successful, Captain White's men were eventually forced to withdraw given shortages of reinforcements and bombs. During the 27th September it was decided that 53 Brigade's attack, from Zollern Trench, to take the

Troops of the Border Regiment rest within the shattered confines of Thiepval Wood during the late summer of 1916.

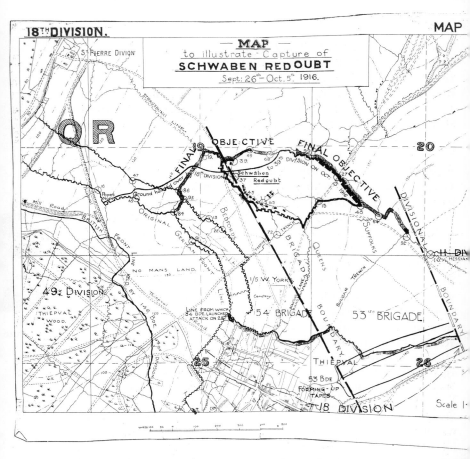

Map 17. This map shows the fighting for Schwaben Redoubt, 26th September 1916, involving many units of the 18th Division.

Schwaben Redoubt would be called for at 1.00 pm on 28th September. This was bound to be a terribly difficult fight against determined defenders.

 This attack was launched from a series of forming up tapes astride that portion of Zollern Trench which faced north-west towards Bulgar Trench. The left boundary of 53 Brigade was four hundred yards due east of the church. The Brigade frontage was five hundred yards wide with the 8th Suffolks on the right and the 7th Queen's (attached from 55 Brigade) on their left. To the left of 53 Brigade two companies of the 7th Bedfordshires (54 Brigade) would attack past the communal cemetery and parallel to the original German front line. Their objective was a position between the Schwaben Redoubt and the German front lines on the west of the redoubt.

At 1.00 pm the events began to unfold well. Bulgar Trench fell easily but beyond there the Germans fought stoutly in the Mouquet Switch trenches, which the Official History and other accounts confusingly refer to as the 'Midway Line'. Ninety minutes after the attack had started the Suffolks were at the east end of Schwaben, at R.20.c.4.5, in touch with advanced units of the 11th Division, but the Queen's were rather too far left and stuck, about the Crucifix at R.19.d.9.3., under the fire from the Redoubt. This situation was resolved in great part by the action of Captain Longbourne who won the DSO. in bombing his way into the south face of the redoubt, at R.19.d.6.5. The Bedfordshires on the left had worked forward past the north of the communal cemetery and were being re-inforced by their support companies and by the 1/5th West Yorkshires (of 49th Division). Two hours after the start of these operations the Queen's held a footing in the southern portion and south-western corner of the Redoubt whilst north-west of the communal cemetery men fought for possession of the numerous strong-points in the old German front line system. The fighting was hand to hand with no quarter given by either side. Gradually the redoubt's defenders were exhausted and killed. By 5.00 pm the Queen's controlled the whole of the southern face of the Schwaben Redoubt whilst a few yards to their left the Bedfordshires and West Yorkshires gradually took control of the western face of the Redoubt by 8.00 pm, Second-Lieutenant Adlam again distinguishing himself amidst this fighting. This magnificent effort was supported by men of 11th Lancashire Fusiliers who crossed No Man's Land, secured part of the German front lines and then worked eastwards to join with the soldiers of 54 Brigade now on the west of Schwaben Redoubt. Throughout the night a series of bombing raids were launched against the British troops clinging to the redoubt and the north-western tip was lost at approximately 7.30 am on the morning of 29th.

On the right of 18th Division the 11th Division now redoubled its efforts to capture Stuff Redoubt and Hessian trench to the east of it. A further assault was ordered for 29th September during which Stuff Redoubt again held out but the portion of Hessian Trench between Stuff Redoubt and the Mouquet Switch trench (Midway Line) fell. During this day the 18th Division's troops reorganized, bringing 55 Brigade into the line and the following day, 30th September, fought throughout along the south and west faces of the Schwaben Redoubt. That afternoon at 4.00 pm, the 11th Division finally succeeded in securing all of the southern part of Stuff Redoubt, the extraordinary bravery of Captain White being rewarded when his men finally overcame the German resistance and consolidated their hard won gains there. The citation for Archie White's Victoria Cross explains that he: 'was in command of the troops that held the southern and western faces of a redoubt. For four days and nights by his indomitable spirit, great personal courage, and skilful dispositions, he held his position under heavy fire of all kinds and against several counter-attacks. Though short of supplies and ammunition, his determination never wavered. When the enemy attacked in greatly superior numbers and had almost ejected our troops from the redoubt, he personally led a counter-attack, which finally cleared the enemy out of the southern and western faces. He risked his life continually, and was the life and soul of the defence.'[3]

That night the troops of 11th Division were relieved by the 25th Division. During the period 26th-30th September the casualty returns of 11th Division showed as 143 officers and 3,472 other ranks, almost 30 per cent of those being killed.

On the 18th Divisional front the position was desperate. The northern face of the redoubt had been taken and then lost as had the north-west corner, as far as R.19.d.3.7. All the battalions were exhausted by the severity of the fighting, the foul stench and proximity of death and the sucking mud which clogged every trench. The constant shelling and trench mortar explosions had reduced the terrain to an unrecognizable pulp, within which the deep

This sketch shows the bombardment falling on Schwaben Redoubt during the actions which took place on October 12th, 1916.

dugouts were full of wounded and dying men who could not be got out by the stretcher bearers. During the period 1st October to the 5th October the 18th Division fought itself to a standstill in holding the bulk of Schwaben Redoubt. During that period there were numerous German counter attacks using minenwerfer, grenade, gas and flammenwerfer but, when the 18th Division were relieved by the 39th Division on 5th October, only a tiny fraction of the redoubt in the north-western corner remained in German hands. The ground handed over to the 39th Division also included the section of the original German front line running along to the Pope's Nose.

The effective capture of the Schwaben position had cost the 18th Division almost 2,000 casualties, eighty officers and 1,910 other ranks. Between Stuff Redoubt and Schwaben the British now had observation past the Ancre Valley and northwards, a situation which seriously undermined German morale and effectiveness in that area of the Somme battlefield. Regrettably the remaining portion of the redoubt took a further nine days to overcome, at the end of which period the 39th Division's narrative sought to take credit for the capture of Schwaben.

The Final Clearance of Schwaben and Stuff Redoubts

At 4.30 am, on the 9th October the 16th Sherwood Foresters made a surprise attack on the portion of the north face of Schwaben Redoubt still controlled by the Germans. Although they gained the trench, in so far as it was distinguishable, they were forced to withdraw later. Fortunately the position in this area was then dramatically improved when the 10th Cheshires, 7 Brigade, 25th Division, overran the remaining positions on the north face of Stuff Redoubt at 12.35 pm. These men then pushed posts to the north east and along the old German second positions in the direction of Grandcourt from where they repulsed German counter attacks that evening. During the next four days these positions were secured by other units of 25th Division and further outposts were pushed forwards as a result of a successful attack at 2.45 pm on 14th October by the 8th Loyal North Lancashires, to gain observation down the Stump Road over Grandcourt for the first time.

The German counter attacks at Stuff redoubt saw the death of 21 year old Captain Ted Underhill of the 8th Loyal North Lancs. After the war an account of his service and death entitled *A Year on the Western Front* was edited by Sydney Milledge and published in 1924. In that account we are told that, on the night of the 12th,

C Company, commanded by Underhill, was holding the north face of the redoubt. A Company, commanded by Underhill's close friend Captain Tindall Atkinson, was in support. During the afternoon a period of unnatural calm had developed and it seemed that a German attack might be imminent. The assault which Underhill and his men suffered was made along Stump Road and the old German fire and support trenches leading into the northern face of the Redoubt (at R.21.c.1.8 and 3.8).

'The three attacks were simultaneous and at point 18 every man defending the post was killed. The first warning to Captain Underhill was a shower of bombs. There were two entrances to the dug-out and bombs came down each flight of steps causing casualties among his men.'

In the ensuing fighting Ted Underhill rushed up the steps and rallied his men in the defence of the redoubt. An SOS barrage was ordered from A Company's headquarters, which already knew

that many casualties had been experienced by C Company in front. To the right there was the sound of many Lewis guns and overhead the scene was illuminated by the Verey lights and flares which both sides were sending skywards. Eventually the accuracy of the SOS barrage enabled Tindall Atkinson's men to regain control over the bombing block at R.21.c.1.8. It was just thirty yards to the rear where Ted Underhill had established his company headquarters and he had been killed by a grenade splinter which had penetrated his skull beneath his steel helmet. His body was found, by his comrade Tindall Atkinson, and is now buried in Ovillers Military Cemetery.

**Captain Ted Underhill
8th Loyal North Lancs**

Just to the west the 39th Division completed the clearance of Schwaben on 14th October. The northern limits of the redoubt were attacked by the 4/5th Black Watch and the 1/1st Cambridgeshires whilst the left positions were taken and advanced by the 1/6th Cheshires. 2nd Lieutenant Bob Morton of the 1/6th Cheshires remembered the scene, seventy years on:

'The nearest thing to hell. Absolute murder. Some good dugouts there. We were in one half of the Schwaben and the other half was still German. The shellfire was shocking. The land was six feet lumps of clay and chalk   and dead with green faces. Unburied dead lay all over Thiepval. I talked to one of the dead who was standing up in a trench, leaning

A single German corpse, one of the many hundreds of dead who fell during the battle for Thiepval and Schwaben.

up against a side. I asked him a question. The front of his pocket came away in my hand.'[4]

Today the Schwaben Redoubt is undoubtedly the unmarked grave of many hundreds of soldiers, both British and German, whose bodies were never and could never be recovered from such desolation. That October the gruesome process of clearing the battlefield of those bodies which could be found went on continuously until, in November, the battles for control of the St Pierre Divion defences below Schwaben began.

The Battle of the Ancre Heights (21st October) and the fall of St Pierre Divion (November 13th)

Although Thiepval and the surrounding redoubts had fallen, the old German front lines north of the Mill Road still remained intact. East of Schwaben the Germans still occupied Stuff Trench which ran eastwards and crossed Stump Road, beyond which it was named Regina Trench. An enormous attack on 21st October all along the Ancre Heights on a frontage of 5,000 yards, involving four divisions with the support of 200 heavy guns and howitzers as well as the artillery of seven divisions, saw the fall of Stuff Trench and Regina Trench as far as the Pys to Courcelette Road. The events here were observed in detail by Edmund Blunden whose division, the 39th, was due to attack both to the east and west of Schwaben Redoubt. Moving up from Aveluy to the scene of his men's forthcoming attack Blunden recalled the images within Blighty Valley with graphic clarity. This was a walk and setting which thousands of British soldiers had witnessed and endured in the preceding weeks.

'...we found ourselves filing up a valley under the noses of howitzers standing black and burnished in the open, and loosing off with deadly clamour while the bare-chested gunners bawled and blasphemed " Happy Valley or Blighty Valley, which was it? Farther along stood Authuille Wood, and we went in along a tram-line and a board walk, whereon with sweating foreheads and sharp voices some Highland officers were numbering off some of the most exhausted men (just relieved) I had ever seen. Near here was the captured German work called Leipzic Redoubt, with its underworld comforts, from bakehouse to boudoir; our companies were accommodated there, while the battalion headquarters entered he greasy, rotting shanties of typical British sandbags and tinware in the Wood, at a spot called Tithe Barn, and the night came on.'[5]

The following morning after an uncomfortable night Blunden and his companion Cassels took a party of men forward to the assembly positions from which they would launch their attack the following day.

'The walk to the front line lay over the most bewildering battlefield, so gouged and hummocked, so denatured and dun, so crowded with brown shrapnel cases and German long-handled grenades, shell-holes, rifles, water-bottles; a billowing desert; and yet there was not much opportunity or reason for contemplating this satire in iron brown and field grey, for the staff-supplied motive of "offensive operations" was not yet weakening, and a rough road was being made here, and limbers were tipping and clattering ahead there, and guns being hauled forward, and signallers running out their lines and burying their cables, and little strings of burdened soldiers like mine trickling onward until they passed tragi-comically among those black accidents and emanations on the skyline.'[6]

Once the attack, which these preparations supported, had been

Hot dinner rations being issued from Field Kitchens in the Ancre area during October.

undertaken Blunden's men were relieved from the surroundings of Stuff Trench. His description of that desolate, frosted and saturated location is a powerful and tragic one.

'It was Geoffrey Salter speaking out firmly in the darkness. Stuff Trench-this was Stuff Trench; three feet deep, corpses under foot, corpses on the parapet. He told us, while shell after shell slipped in crescendo wailing into the vibrating ground, that his brother had been killed, and he had buried him; Doogan had been wounded, gone downstairs into one of the dugout shafts after hours of sweat, and a shell came downstairs to finish him; "and" says he, "you can get a marvellous view of Grandcourt from this trench. We've been looking at it all day".'

The whole of the Thiepval crest was now in British hands for the first time, although, as you will see from these positions yourself, it was impossible to see into the nearside of the Ancre Valley because of the convex slope of the land here. Sheltered from view at the foot of that slope was an embankment, roughly twelve feet high in most places although more than fifty feet high at St Pierre

Divion, and containing a warren of deep dugouts many of which were interconnected.

Rather than repeat the frontal attacks across Mill Road which had proved so disastrous on 1st July it was decided to take St Pierre Divion by an assault from above, in this case down those convex slopes from Schwaben astride the Divion Road. By this stage in the Somme campaign the weather had exerted a terrible impact upon the terrain and these actions as part of the Battle of the Ancre are generally recognized as having been undertaken in some of the most ghastly and inhuman circumstances wrought by the war.

The Fall of St Pierre Divion during the Battle of the Ancre

Since the 8th November much colder weather had settled across the north of France. The ground was softened and the battered trenches had filled with glutinous chalk. The men had been exposed to constant, exhausting carrying duties in the wet at the front and to overcrowded and filthy billets when further back. The officers felt that any more rain would make infantry progress impossible. Observing the situation from Schwaben Redoubt Edmund Blunden noted that:

> 'Sluggish, soaking mists, or cold stinging wind, loaded the air and the spirit of man; the ruins of the world looked black and unalterable; Thiepval Wood's ghostly gallows-trees made no sound nor movement. Thus, then, beyond doubt, the gigantic clangour of the Somme offensive had ceased, and once or twice one heard it urged that Caesar went into winter quarters. The fog, dewing one's khaki, scarcely let the sun rise, and the grey chalky mud, as though to claim the only victory, crawled down the dugout entrances, whether those still had stairs, or were mere gullets, their woodwork burnt out by phosphorous bombs or shells.'

In fact Blunden's hope that the 'gigantic clangour of the Somme offensive had ceased' was mistaken. The Battle of the Ancre was about to begin and his division, the 39th, would be at its centre.

North of the Ancre the attack would be delivered by V Corps and south by two divisions of II Corps, the 39th Division, who would attack St Pierre Divion, with the 19th Division on its right as a flank guard. The date set was the 13th November. We can concentrate upon the attack of two battalions, the 4/5th Black Watch and the 1/6th Cheshires. The Cheshires were expected to roll up the Strassburg Line, which ran in a north-westerly direction along the old Divion road, before entering and taking the village itself. On their left the 4/5th Black Watch would take the old

Two photographs showing the Ancre valley and St. Pierre Divion during November 1916.

'A Fag after a Fight.'

German front line, parallel to Strassburg, running to the north of the Mill Road down to the river.

Their assembly had been undertaken in moonlight during the early hours, but as time passed the clear conditions gave way to a dank and dripping fog which saturated every item of the men's kit. The assembly positions were merely blown in trenches and any suitable shell hole. The barrage was arranged for 5.45 am but observers knew little of its effect since visibility was little more than thirty yards. There was still ninety minutes of darkness to be negotiated when the advance got underway. The men were supported by three tanks, one of which became stuck before it reached Thiepval. The second quickly stopped with mechanical trouble but the third did fight its way down the German front line and from there into the Strassburg line where it ditched after causing the collapse of a dugout.

Behind that tank the infantry had terrible problems keeping a bearing. The dense fog and cratered ground meant that no adequate landmark could be seen from which to fix a direction. Snipers and isolated machine guns took their toll, especially amongst the Black Watch, and it was a slow and haphazard advance which took these two battalions down to the banks above the Ancre. Here the Black Watch met with men of the 16th Sherwood Foresters who had attacked up the Ancre valley at 6.15 am, and overrun the dugouts within the embankment. This combined force then swept north-

These two photographs show a portion of the vast amount of material captured during the taking of St Pierre Divion.

eastwards and met with the Chesires as they entered and captured what little was left of St Pierre Divion at about 7.40 am. One lighter note was struck by a signaller of 1/6th Cheshires who had entered the wreckage with instructions to look out for suitable supplies of wire in a Brigade Signals dugout. He sent back the message, 'Brigade Signals ain't here, wire isn't here, and St Pierre Divion isn't here'![7]

During their attack the Cheshires had captured 150 prisoners and numerous items of equipment including two machine guns. Their casualties were three officers killed and twenty-nine men who were either killed or died of wounds. Nine were missing and there were 126 wounded. In the context of other attacks around Thiepval and the Schwaben the Cheshires had escaped lightly. The 4/5th Black Watch had also suffered relatively light casualties in the context of what had been achieved. This battalion and the 16th Sherwood Foresters had made so many captures that at one stage British troops within the Ancre valley were in danger of being outnumbered by their prisoners. By nightfall the 39th Division's cage held the best part of 1,000 prisoners, and more would follow, and it seemed as if the willpower of the Germans had come to an end in this part of the battle-front. That night the Black Watch began the consolidation of parts of the Hansa Lines whilst the Cheshires took over all the St Pierre Divion defences along with other strong-points along the Ancre valley. In fact the intensity of the cold and wet weather which had now descended in full spate would soon force the abandonment of the Ancre campaign. The following spring the German Army pulled back to new positions in the Hindenburg line, handing over the now indefensible villages of Grandcourt, Miraumont, Irles and beyond. Undoubtedly the unremitting struggles for and the eventual success gained at Thiepval, Schwaben Redoubt and above the Ancre was a key factor in ensuring that that decision was forced upon the German Army.

1. Public Record Office, WO95/2015.
2. Public Record Office, WO95/2015.
3. London Gazette. 26 October 1916.
4. David Kelsall. Tape recorded interview.
5. Tithebarn was a trench at the head of Dumbarton Track looking across the old No Man's Land at the south of Leipzig Redoubt. There were deep dug-outs on Tithebarn, just behind Boggart Hole Clough, at R.1.a.7.2.
6. *Undertones of War*, Edmund Blunden, 1928.
7. *War History of the 6th Cheshires*, Charles Smith 1932.

Chapter Five
BROTHERS IN ARMS

One of the abiding features of personal recollections and memoirs drawing upon the Great War is the intense respect, sympathy and deep friendship which grew amongst those who shared and recorded its ultimate horror. 'The splendid fellowship which we shared has been for most of us the greatest thing in our lives. If we have any pride, it is that once we were accounted worthy of that fellowship.' So wrote one young man not then entitled to vote but who served here at Thiepval.[1] Many contemporary chronicles of the war have a stark brevity which, quite understandably, cuts away all superfluous matter from the soldiers' issues of honour, bravery, fortitude and sacrifice. Other accounts have reached a literary quality which will seldom be surpassed. However, it would be an incomplete image if we painted Thiepval's likeness without blemish. In this chapter I have tried to draw together some of the personalities whose actions, sometimes undertaken as fine and honest endeavour and sometimes with fragile human failing, have revealed the truth of war as fought here at Thiepval.

The shooting of Private Crozier

The events which brought Percy Crozier to the command of the 9th Royal Irish Rifles are well documented in his memoir, *A Brass Hat in No Man's Land*.[2] However, under the Lieutenant-Colonel's command was another Crozier, Rifleman 9/14218 James Crozier of A Company, who was no relation but nevertheless was known to and dependant upon his Commanding Officer. Since James' enlistment at the age of seventeen, when the then Major had given an undertaking to James' mother to look after her youthful son's interests, the two soldiers had realized that they shared little apart from a surname. Perhaps that would not have been surprising given the social gulf which usually existed between many officers and the other ranks whom they commanded. However, in this particular case the relationship took a tragic and unpredictable turn after the 9th Royal Irish Rifles landed in France on 3rd October 1915.

At the end of the first fortnight in February 1916 Percy Crozier was asked his opinion on the young rifleman's worth. His response would largely seal the fate of James Crozier who had by then been found guilty, when on active service, of 'deserting His Majesty's Service'. Percy Crozier's words, written on 15th February, were damning, claiming that James Crozier's crime was deliberately committed with a view to avoiding duty in one of the two small British salients, known as William and Mary Redan, in front of

Hamel below Thiepval. 'From a fighting point of view this soldier is of no value. His behaviour has been that of a "shirker" for the past three months.' In his comments Percy Crozier referred to the case of an officer of the same regiment, Second-Lieutenant Annandale, who had also been tried on a charge of desertion, and found guilty, but whose sentence had been quashed as a result of the intervention of friends with prestige and authority. He implied this had set the wrong precedent and had therefore encouraged rifleman Crozier in the belief that he could escape a charge of desertion without undue penalty.

Twenty four hours earlier, on 14th February, the Field General Court Martial had met to consider the evidence.[3] The accused had entered a plea of not guilty. The members of the court were Major Burnand of the 8th R.I.R., Captain Gaffikin of the 9th R.I.R., and Lieutenant Blackwood of the 8th R.I.R., who heard Crozier's section commander, Corporal Todd, and CSM Arthur Hill, who both agreed that he had been identified as missing from duty on the evening of 31st January. In response to both men's evidence Rifleman Crozier 'declined to cross examine this witness'. This

Douglas Haig

inability or reluctance of the defendant to engage in any sort of cross examination, allied to his lack of access to any military/legal defence or a 'soldier's friend', must throw an enormous doubt upon the impartiality of the court and the fairness of its subsequent decisions. However, faced with Crozier's silence the court continued and then heard from a Corporal Taylor of the 7th Ammunition Sub Park who stated that he apprehended Rifleman Crozier on 4th February at the park's Transport lines. Taylor claimed that the equipmentless and hapless Crozier had admitted, at the time of his detention, to being a deserter, although no witness corroborated that assertion. Again James Crozier declined the chance to cross examine this witness and also the subsequent witness, a military policeman who had returned the rifleman to the 36th Division's HQ, who had described Crozier's behaviour on that fateful journey as 'peculiar'. More than eighty years on such behaviour seems quite understandable, whatever meaning that word 'peculiar' was meant to convey!

In his defence Rifleman Crozier was recorded as saying that, on the night in question, 'I went into the front line trenches with my platoon. I was feeling very ill; with pains all over me. I do not remember what I did. I was dazed: I do not remember being warned for any duty. I cannot remember leaving the trenches even.' There followed a perfunctory cross-examination by the court whose purpose seems to have been to entice Crozier into admitting that he should have reported sick beforehand, thereby, had he done so, improving his chances of being found not guilty. Prejudicial evidence of character was then shown to the court, describing Crozier as 'Bad' and identifying that he had also been absent from a working party and from his billet in the recent past.

Having received Percy Crozier's clear recommendation the court then found James Crozier guilty as charged and no pleas were made to commute the sentence of death. The Commander in Chief confirmed the sentence on 23rd February, *pour encourager les autres*. James Crozier was shot at 7.05 am as the sun rose on the morning of 27th February 1916, four weeks to the day after he had left his comrades at the Redans opposite Beaucourt. On the day of his execution the soldier was still in reality a boy, eighteen years of age and technically ineligible to serve abroad with the British Army. James Crozier was buried at Mailly-Maillet, the place of

Percy Crozier photographed after his promotion to the rank of Brigadier-General in 1916.

his execution, but after the war his body was disinterred and taken for re-burial at the Sucrerie Military Cemetery at Colincamps.

Two other men from this Brigade were also shot at dawn. They were Rifleman McCracken and Rifleman Templeton, both of the 15th Royal Irish Rifles who were executed together on 19th March 1916. They were buried at Mailly-Maillet Communal Cemetery Extension.

In the twenty years before the Great War Percy Crozier had been something of a colonial adventurer. During this period he had both established and cured a drink problem. He returned to

Headstone of Rifleman James Crozier Sucrerie Cemetery, Colincamps.

Britain in 1912 and soon became active in the recruitment and development of the Special Service Section of the West Belfast Regiment of the UVF. Crozier was therefore an active Loyalist and would have described himself as a necessarily severe leader.

A British firing squad in operation 'somewhere in Flanders'.
Right: Douglas Haig's final signature on the warrant which ensured that Rifleman Crozier would be shot at dawn by his comrades in arms.

Once these men had been incorporated within the British Army, Crozier set about their training in his capacity as second-in-command of the 9th Royal Irish Rifles, the Shankhill lads of the 'West Belfast Volunteers', with a hugely energetic zeal. 'We concentrate on two things at the outset; knocking the beer and politics out of all ranks and building up an *esprit-de-corps* in its place.' He regarded it as axiomatic that all soldiers should have the kindly streak of civilized behaviour removed, it being 'necessary to corrode his mentality with bitter-sweet vice and to keep him up to the vicious scratch on all occasions.' Once on active service Crozier continued this harsh but ordered bearing towards his men. Certainly the decision to execute his namesake was an impersonal expedient but it nevertheless fell to Percy Crozier to supervise the arrangements for the promulgation of the sentence and its execution. By midnight on 26th February the condemned man was plied with an excess of liquor, so ending his last chance of a dignified departure on the morrow. The supervising officer, who would be expected to extinguish life if the firing party were to fail, was ordered to dine with his CO in order to 'minimise the chance of his flying to the bottle for support'. The following morning, at Mailly-Maillet, the 9th Battalion of the Royal Irish Rifles were drawn up to hear the sentence carried out. There was snow on the ground and Lieutenant Colonel Crozier witnessed the scene from

SCHEDULE.

Date 14th February 1916. No. 93.

Name of Alleged Offender (a)	Offence charged	Plea	Finding, and if Convicted, Sentence (b)	How dealt with by Confirming Officer
No 9/14218 Rifleman [illegible]es Crozier 9th R. Ir. Rifles	When on active service deserting His Majesty's service	not guilty	Guilty. DEATH	Reserved [illegible]

[illegible]533. [illegible] Army.

Confirmed
D. Haig. Gen
23 Feb 16

Certified that above proceedings have been promulgated and that the sentence was was duly executed at 7.5. a.m on 27th February 1916 – [illegible signature]

Major General
28th Feb. 1916 } Comdg. 36th Division

(a) If the name of the person charged is unknown, he may be described as unknown, with such addition as will identify him.

(b) Recommendation to mercy to be inserted in this column.

[illegible signature] Brig Gen
Comd 107th Inf Bde
Convening Officer.

[illegible signature] Maj
R. Ir. Rifles
President.

his vantage point above the villa wall. His account is a graphic and wretched indictment of inhumanity:

'...the victim is carried to the stake. He is far too drunk to walk. He is out of view save for myself, as I stand on a mound near the wall. As he is produced I see he is practically lifeless and quite unconscious. He has already been bound with ropes. There are hooks on the post; we always do things thoroughly in the Rifles. He is hooked on like dead meat in the butcher's shop... This is war.'

If the account was written in the hope that it would ease the pain of Rifleman Crozier's family, by the knowledge that he knew nothing of what was happening in his final moments, it surely failed to do so.

But Colonel Crozier's stern indifference would stand him in good stead as an observer of, and participant in, the events of 1st July. These events initially occurred at the head of Elgin Avenue after he has led his men forward and then watched his Shankhill Lads dash across the sunken part of Thiepval road during a fortunate lull in the German shelling and machine-gun fire. Crozier certainly lacked nothing in terms of self belief yet paid scant attention to the dreadful sufferings of the men under his command. The resultant account paints a florid, often distasteful, picture and reveals what Crozier certainly deemed the essential insensibility of the man in command.

'This spirited dash ... has cost us fifty dead and seventy disabled. The dead no longer count. War has no use for dead men. With luck they will be buried later; the wounded try to crawl back to our lines. Some are hit again in so doing, but the majority lie out all day, sun-baked, parched, uncared for, often delirious and at any rate in great pain. My immediate duty is to look after the situation and not bother about wounded men. I send a message to brigade and move to my battle headquarters in the wood. It is a deep dug-out which has been allocated to me for my use. It needs to be deep to keep out heavy stuff. The telephone lines are all cut by shellfire. Kelly, a burly six-feet-two-inches-high Irish Nationalist, has been sent in a week before to look after emergency rations. He has endured the preliminary bombardment for a week already with the dead and dying, during which time he has had difficulty going outside, even at night and then only between the shells. A wrong thing has been done. I find the place full of dead and wounded men. It has been used as a refuge. None of the wounded can walk.

116

There are no stretchers. Most are in agony. They have seen no doctor. Some have been there for days. They have simply been pushed down the steep thirty-feet-deep entrance out of further harm's way and left − perhaps forgotten. As I enter the dug-out I am greeted with the most awful cries from these dreadfully wounded men. Their removal is a Herculean task, for it was never intended that the dying and the helpless should have to use the deep stairway. After a time, the last sufferer and the last corpse are removed. Meanwhile I mount the parapet to observe. The attack on the right has come to a standstill; the last detailed man has sacrificed himself on the German wire to the God of War. Thiepval village is masked with a wall of corpses.'

The Victoria Cross has a unique place in the history of military endeavour and bravery, it being the highest award given within Great Britain's armed forces. Since its institution in 1856 the cross has been granted for actions 'in the presence of the enemy' by serving men or officers who 'shall have then performed some signal act of valour or devotion to their country'[4]. In what was, in the mid 19th century, a society dominated by a non elected aristocracy of which the Queen was the unchallenged apex, the Victoria Cross was given an egalitarian character which adds greatly to the appeal and sentiment behind the award. The warrant specified that, 'with a view to place all persons on an equal footing in relation to eligibility for the decoration, that neither rank, nor long service, nor wounds, nor any other circumstance or condition whatsoever, save the merit of conspicuous bravery, shall be held to establish a sufficient claim to the honour.'

Four Victoria Crosses were awarded to men serving with the 36th (Ulster) Division during the actions north-west of Thiepval on 1st July 1916. Whilst that was not in itself unique, for example six were awarded to the 1st Battalion of the Lancashire Fusiliers at Helles during the Gallipoli landings in 1915, but the awards were a matter of enormous pride to all Ulstermen. Two were awarded to men whose deeds were undertaken north of the River Ancre, Geoffrey St George Shillington Cather of the 9th Royal Irish Fusiliers and Rifleman Robert Quigg of the 12th Royal Irish Rifles, whose bravery therefore falls outside the scope of this book. However, the valour of Billy McFadzean and Eric Bell are detailed, rather inadequately in view of their huge contribution and ultimate sacrifice, below.

Not very far, perhaps just a few yards, from the spot where Percy Crozier witnessed the events of 1st July the first Victoria

Rifleman R. Quigg

Lt G St George S Cather

117

Cross awarded during the Somme campaign was won. As with many such awards the medal was given not for effectiveness in killing the enemy but in the risks and sacrifice undertaken in saving fellow life.

Billy McFadzean was born at Lurgan in County Armagh of middle class parents. He was a member of the Ulster volunteers (1st Battalion Ballynafeigh and Newtownbreda, East Belfast Regiment) and later joined the 14th Battalion of the Royal Irish Rifles, with whom he trained as a bomber. Such men were sometimes referred to by their comrades as 'the suicide club' because of the inherent danger and unreliability of the grenades they used.

Just before 7.00 am on the morning of the Great Push the 14th Royal Irish Rifles' bombers were waiting in Whitechurch Street astride Elgin Avenue. They were the immediate support to 109 Brigade's assault battalions. The battalion was due to attack across Thiepval Road towards the Schwaben Redoubt and Billy McFadzean was listening intently as the bombardment reached its shrieking height. The men's nerves were strained and amidst this holocaust of noise and terror the mills bombs were being distributed. This was the moment when catastrophe struck. As another case was being opened the box of bombs slipped from Billy's grasp and two fell to the floor, their safety pins inadvertently detached. Without hesitation Billy McFadzean threw himself across the bombs to shelter his friends from the inevitable explosion.

Private McFadzean's action undoubtedly saved many lives, although three men nearby did suffer wounds. Billy McFadzean's remains were removed by stretcher bearers and it is said that many of his comrades wept openly in their anguish that such bravery should have been rewarded with such a squalid end. Those remains were placed behind the lines prior to the assault, to await collection when time permitted. Unfortunately, and like so many hundreds of other men belonging to the units which fought here at Thiepval that day, Billy McFadzean's remains were never identified and he is commemorated on the Thiepval Memorial which overlooks the site of his last self sacrificial action. The most likely place of burial is in fact within yards of Private McFadzean's last act, within the Connaught Cemetery which has 642 'unknown' graves.

One footnote of interest surrounded the presentation ceremony at Buckingham Palace which took place on the last day in February, 1917. In presenting the medal to Billy's father, a Belfast Justice of the Peace, the King rightly said that, 'nothing finer has been done in this war for which I have yet given the Victoria Cross,

Private
McFadzean

than the act performed by your son in giving his life so heroically to save the lives of comrades.' In recognition the dead soldier's father had been granted a third class railway ticket with which to make the return journey to Belfast.

Eric Bell came from a family which was steeped in military tradition. His parents were Captain Edward Bell and Dora Algeo Bell. Although Eric was born in Enniskillen the bulk of his education had been in northern England at Warrington and later at Liverpool University where he studied architecture under the guidance of Professor Sir Charles Reilly. The citation for his award makes very clear how far above and beyond the call of duty Captain Bell's actions went:

'For most conspicuous bravery. He was in command of a Trench Mortar Battery, and advanced with the infantry in the attack. When our front line was hung up by enfilading machine-gun fire, Capt. Bell crept forward and shot the machine gunner. Later, on no less than three occasions, when our bombing parties, which were clearing the enemy's trenches, were unable to advance, he went forward alone and threw trench-mortar bombs among the enemy. When he had no more bombs available, he stood on the parapet, under intense fire, and used a rifle with great coolness and effect

119

on the enemy advancing to counter attack. Finally, he was killed rallying and reorganizing infantry parties which had lost their officers. All this was outside the scope of his normal duties with his battery. He gave his life in his supreme devotion to duty.'

Captain Eric Bell

One candid and telling tribute came from Liverpool University where Professor Reilly said of Captain Bell that he was 'one of the few men I know who could... have won such an honour without being spoilt by it.' An interesting note was struck by the Bell family's record of service with the 9th Royal Inniskilling Fusiliers. When Eric was posted to this battalion his father was already serving as adjutant and Eric's two brothers, Alan George Frankland Bell and Haldane Frankland Bell, travelled from America and Australia to serve with the same unit.

Sergeant J Turnbull

So far the personalities which we have considered have been involved further north. By contrast James Turnbull was engaged to the south of the village at Leipzig Redoubt and this location will always be associated in visitor's minds with the Highland Light Infantry's Service battalions from Scotland's great industrial city.

James Turnbull was born in 1883 and passed through his childhood in Glasgow where he was educated. On leaving school James was employed in the tailoring trade. Having joined the 17th HLI on the outbreak of the war his intelligence, fine physique and determined manner ensured that he quickly rose to the rank of Sergeant. The final act in the story of James Turnbull is a fascinating one to follow in the field since the location where his acts of great bravery, which gave him a posthumous Victoria Cross, and his known grave are within easy reach of both Thiepval and Authuille.

The 17th HLI were part of 97 Brigade's assault on the Leipzig Redoubt. They attacked from positions to the left and right of Campbell Avenue, that is the lane which today runs eastwards from Authuille to the cross roads just south of the Granatloch. On their left their sister battalion, the 16th HLI made little progress but the 17th Battalion's men swept into the German front trenches either side of The Naze, securing the south-western corner of the salient. It was here that James Turnbull took note of a large but abandoned bomb store. As the day wore on the 17th HLI's position was constantly threatened by its exposed position, having made no permanent advance past the German support trenches here. Whilst the 17th HLI held on in the Leipzig Redoubt a succession of further battalions, the 11th Border, the 1st Dorsets and the

19th Lancashire Fusiliers, made futile attempts to cross the fire swept zone from the north of Authuille Wood around Chowbent Street and Chequerbent Street.

Meanwhile, constant German bombing attacks were made against the 17th HLI. These came from the 'Bull's Eye', just north of the Granatloch, and from strong-points A5 and A4 to the east of the Glasgow men where the German trenches on the southern face of the redoubt had not been assaulted in the first wave of attacks that morning. Throughout this period Turnbull behaved magnificently, his height and strength enabling him to outdistance the German bombers who attacked from the Bull's Eye area. Throughout the early morning small parties of men from 14 Brigade struggled into the Redoubt to re-enforce the 17th HLI. For upwards of fourteen hours Turnbull maintained this position and almost single-handedly saved his battalion from being outflanked. During this time the German stick grenades were also utilized when Mills Bomb supplies ran short. It was during the evening that Jimmy Turnbull met his death at the hands of a sniper who shot him as he bombed forward from the Granatloch in opposition to a counter attack developing from the German support trenches to the north.

Turnbull's Victoria Cross citation is as much a testimony to the bravery of the band of men who aided and supported Turnbull as it is to his extraordinary courage that day:

'Although his party was wiped out and replaced several times during the day, Sergeant Turnbull never wavered in his determination to hold the post, the loss of which would have been very serious. Almost single-handed, he maintained his position, and displayed the highest degree of valour and skill in the performance of his duties.'

James Turnbull VC, is buried at the Lonsdale Cemetery just a few hundred yards from the scene of his last actions. The foothold which he and his comrades gained and then held was the most northerly permanent bite into German held territory on this first day of the Somme battle. Once it had fallen the process of consolidation and enlargement began and it was from just north of here that the successful attack on the village of Thiepval was launched, in late September, by men of the 18th Division.

By contrast with Jimmy Turnbull, whose memory is best preserved by his bravery and the eloquence of his actions, two writer-soldiers who served at Thiepval have secured the image of the Great War here in quietly reflective prose. Their words contrast with the somewhat brusque, blunt and 'gung-ho' style of Percy Crozier. The first of these men was Charles Douie whose memoir,

The Weary Road, recalls his service which was mainly spent with the 1st Battalion of the Dorsetshire Regiment, a regular unit which was brigaded with service battalions from Salford, Manchester and Glasgow. Douie's work was published in October 1929. This was a time when disenchantment with the course and consequences of the Great War were running high, yet Douie's determination to record the soldiers' conviction in the rightness of what they had undertaken came across strongly. The memoir received considerable acclaim and is often taken to reflect the unspoken ordinary soldiers' pride in what they did. In this respect Douie speaks for many in his generation for whom the war was a matter of honour and for whom the concepts of fighting for King, Country and Liberty were clear and unambiguous. Later works by Douie were not so fortunate in their critical reception. The second writer is Edmund Blunden whose understated yet evocative literature stands amongst the very best that was inspired by the Great War.

Charles Douie

Charles Douie was the son of a career officer in the Indian Civil Service. He was a lonely child whose parents could not, of necessity of circumstance, spare him time. He was brought up in boarding schools but had succeeded in gaining a scholarship to Oxford to read History shortly before the outbreak of war. Even though he was little more than an educated but still naive schoolboy, Charles Douie did not hesitate to enlist. He was eighteen years of age and served throughout the war from August 1914 to the close of hostilities.

In describing his fellow officers Charles Douie spoke with simple but moving words about their spirit of honour and willing sacrifice in the face of danger and likely death. In many ways Douie felt that it was always the best who were taken. He was never able to recover from the loss of so many treasured friendships amongst whom he had grown to manhood:

'They sleep, many of them, on the uplands of Picardy. They asked for no reward, no sunlit fields of heaven. They played a man's part, and held their heads high, till Death came in a roaring whirlwind and one more little hour was played. Yet perhaps , as they sleep, they hear a voice across the ages "Well Done".'

In fact Douie realized that many were so tortured by their experience that such men came to welcome the idea and certainty of death. Whilst walking one day with a school-friend and comrade:

2/Lieutenant
C Douie

'I was surprised when he told me that life meant nothing to him, that he had hardly known a happy hour, that he cared very little whether he lived or died. Being very young, I had not previously realised how much of unhappiness the laughter of a brave man may conceal. Death waited for this subaltern on the Somme. He kept his rendezvous without flinching and without dismay. He did not apprehend the majesty, or recognise the dominion, of Death. To him, as to the Guards Ensign in *The Way of Revelation*, Death gave not a summons, but a welcome, "arms wide to embrace, sleep strong to enfold, a friend there faithful and true".'

Like many who had survived the war Charles Douie hoped that some future good could be wrung from the human and material wreckage of the conflict. He and his fellow survivors had already been stung by the bitter condemnation of many whose words in the 1920s portrayed the conflict as ultimately immoral and tragically wasteful. The last sentence of his work is an appeal to us across the distances of time and values which now separate us:

'Perhaps some day later generations may begin to see our war in a truer perspective, and may discern it as an inevitable step in the tragic process by which consciousness has informed the will of man, by which in time all things will be fashioned fair.'

Edmund Blunden

Edmund Blunden's incomparable book, *Undertones of War*,[5] is a memorable and illuminating insight into the life of an officer serving with an infantry battalion, the 11th Royal Sussex, during the Great War. Chapters 10, 11 and 12 of that book deal in detail with the events which unfolded around the Schwaben Redoubt during the autumn of 1916. If you have time, before departing for Thiepval, take the trouble to borrow a copy from your library. Blunden's work is fine literature, poetry and a magnificently sensitive evocation of the sights, sounds and terrors which abounded in Thiepval during late 1916. Often, within the awfulness which abounded, Blunden was able to capture the moments of humour and human warmth which made life more bearable for the combatants. Throughout his work a critical eye is cast towards the high command's concept of 'offensive spirit'. Yet Blunden was a man who did not shirk his duty, but he was sensible and sensitive enough to know that it need not have been this way.

His arrival in the British trench system in the autumnal shadows of Thiepval was as part of an officer's reconnaissance party. Having

123

left his platoons at Martinsart Wood he passed into Aveluy Wood which 'is strangely uninhabited; the moss is rimy, its red leaves make a carpet not a thread less fine than those in King's houses.' Through the wood and along the railway line, where he expected to see the 2.30 for Albert at any moment, Blunden looked out towards Authuille across the Ancre:

> 'A trolley-line crosses, too, but disjointedly: disjointedness now dominates the picture. When we have passed the last muddy pool and derailed truck, we come into a maze of trenches, disjointed indeed; once, plainly, of nice architecture and decoration, now a muddle of torn wire netting and twisted rails, of useless signboards, of foul soaked holes and huge humps − the old British system looking up towards lofty Thiepval.'

Their destination is a dugout at what Blunden refers to as Gordon House (surely Gordon Castle in Thiepval Wood). As they make their way up, 'shell after shell hisses past our heads into the inundations of the Ancre, below this shoulder of brown earth, lifting as high as the hill wild sputtering founts of foam and mud. God! Golly! The next salvo − and here's that dugout. A stained face stares out. "I shouldn't stand there, if I were you: come in." "No, I'm all right: don't want to be in the way." "Come in, blast you; just had two men killed where you are".'

His departure from this area, which had clearly made a huge impact upon him, was also beautifully recorded. In his testimony Blunden recalled how, below Thiepval on that day:

> 'our hearty Quartermaster Swain was with his transport, and in particular he was guarding, with all the skill of years of suspicion and incident, our issue of rum. When he called at headquarters presently, he was distressed, and his "eyes were wild". Two jars of rum had been lifted under his very nose by the infallible Jocks. It was a feat of arms indeed, but poor Swain felt his occupation was gone.'

But now it was the battalion's chance to leave. It was not the same men who had arrived but their joy at going from Thiepval was unconfined:

> '...limbers were soon more than brimful, and we hustled down through Authuille and over Black Horse Bridge, "for ever and ever". The battalion was on the roadside ready to march, and amid humorous and artful glances we fell in. Lancashire Dump in the verge of Aveluy Wood, and the old French fingerposts and notices, and the mossy clear places between the trees, and the straight, damp, firm highway,

good-bye to you all; there in the marsh the wild duck and moorcock noise, and farther behind one hears the stinging lash of shells in the swamp, but we are marching. Not the same "we" who in the golden dusty summer tramped down into the verdant valley, even then a haunt of every leafy spirit and the blue-eyed ephydriads, now Nature's slimy wound with spikes of blackened bone...'

1. Charles Douie, *The Weary Road*
2. Published in 1930 by Jonathan Cape, London. This book is readily available on the second hand market and gives an interesting, often brutal and sometimes eccentric insight into the life of a battalion's officers. Crozier mellowed to become a well known Pacifist in post war years.
3. The documents which this and other similar cases generated are held in the Public Record Office under the file WO 71/450.
4. The Victoria Cross Warrant given at Buckingham Palace on 29th January 1856.
5. First published by Richard Cobden-Sanderson, 1928.

Chapter Six
THE CEMETERIES AND MEMORIALS

This chapter's purpose is to enhance your understanding of the many cemeteries and memorials in this area. All of these commemorative structures and headstones are capable of moving the emotions of visitors, especially those who know at first hand the sacrifice and anguish of the soldier in action. There should be a pride in what was done, tempered with the benefit of our hindsight which ought to ensure that nothing to match the awfulness of 1916 arises again. However, that year did not witness the end of Thiepval's torture and the shock is to see so many graves which relate to the Second Battle of the Somme and subsequent actions to clear Thiepval Ridge.

Whilst looking within many of the cemeteries you will notice the profligate numbers of graves from the 1918 period. These stem from the fighting whose origins lay in the German March Offensive which struck the British Fifth Army outside St Quentin on 21st March. The relative weakness of this army ensured that the German initiative would bring them considerable gains. During the next two weeks these Tommies fell back, never routed but in a state of perpetual harassment and suffering terrible casualties. During this phase the British Army was placed under the overall direction of General Ferdinand Foch, finally bringing some central and co-ordinated control to the conduct of the war's strategy. Bapaume fell on the 25th, Aveluy fell on the night of 26-27th March and Albert soon after. By 5th April the main battle had run its course and the Germans had failed in their attempt to take Amiens or split the French and British. There was severe fighting in Aveluy Wood on 6th April but this presaged a period of calm whilst the Allies gathered themselves for the decisive counter attack. Much of what the German Army had won was, in military terms, a worthless wasteland, the old Somme battlefield and the areas which had been devastated by the Germans during their withdrawal in the spring of 1917.

August marked the turning point of the fighting in the Thiepval area. Since mid-July the Germans had been under pressure. On 8th August a massive Franco-British assault had erupted on the Amiens front. On the 14th August the German retreat from areas north of the Ancre began. On the 15th the British were across the Ancre valley and into Thiepval Wood. On the 21st a major British attack developed north of the Ancre, and on the following day Albert and locations south towards Bray sur Somme were captured.

This photograph purports to show French soldiers within the ruins of Thiepval. In my mind there is some doubt whether this can be Thiepval since the photograph can only have been taken in 1917, after the German withdrawal, or after the summer of 1918. In either case cases it is my opinion that the devastation caused by constant shell-fire would not have left such substantial structures standing upright.

The way was now clear for Thiepval to be retaken and the whole of the ridge was captured on the 24th August. There was little more than two months of the war left to run and within weeks the civilian population would return to begin clearing the devastation and wreckage of four years of warfare. It would be fourteen further years before the Imperial War Graves Commission finished their part of the commemorative work around the village.

THE MEMORIALS

The Thiepval Memorial to the Missing

The Thiepval Memorial to the Missing is an enormously moving and visually distinctive structure. Its aura reaches out across many miles of the surrounding battlefield. Every visitor finds it difficult to decide whether they admire or loathe the architecture. Whatever your choice it is undeniably a chilling reminder of what the war's human cost became. I cannot imagine that, in today's economic and social climate, any memorial of comparable size or design could or should be contemplated. One hopes it would never be needed.

The architect of Thiepval's extraordinary memorial was Sir Edwin Lutyens (1869-1944). He had come to the forefront of British architecture at a time when the Empire was almost at its zenith and when the old Gothic revival in architectural style was losing its momentum. He had developed a prestigious practice and had become the favoured architect for the very rich and wealthy for whom he designed a series of magnificent, romantic country houses all over Britain and Ireland around the turn of the century. By the outbreak of war Lutyens had become, along with Sir Herbert Baker, Britain's premier Imperial architect and had been responsible for many buildings of architectural importance. Most magnificent and flamboyant of all Lutyen's civic work was the Viceroy's Palace at Delhi, now the seat of Government of India. That palace was the ultimate monument of the Raj and indeed of the British Empire. However, even before the war's end the Imperial War Graves Commission had started the process of commissioning architects to design and establish fitting commemorative cemeteries within which the bereaved families would feel that proper tribute had been paid to their loss. After the Great War had ended Lutyens spent much of his time in completing the designing and creation of the dignified and imposing cemeteries located around the Somme battlefield. Some of his purest work is to be found at Serre Road Number Two cemetery which is a reminder of how beautifully Lutyens could execute the Neo-Classical style. This is the largest cemetery on the Somme and contains the graves of 7,139 soldiers. Just to give an example of the range of Lutyen's work you might like to imagine in your mind's eye the intimate and austerely understated lines of the Cenotaph in Whitehall, for which design he was also responsible.

Soon after the war's end many of the small battlefield cemeteries in the immediate vicinity of the Thiepval Memorial had been cleared, even before building work was commenced, the soldier's remains being removed to other locations. The purpose of this was to ensure that the proximity of nearby cemeteries did not detract from the impact of the massive memorial. The unfortunate consequence is that many of the Pals who fought here in July 1916 are buried in locations which are alien to their memory. After Lutyen's designs were accepted the Thiepval Memorial was constructed by the then Imperial War Graves Commission in the four years between 1928 and 1932, the height of one of the world's

Memorial to the Missing
Mill Road Cemetery

Connaught Cemetery

Ulster Towe
Tl

This aerial photograph shows the location of the Ulster Tower in front of Thiepval Wood. Also visible are the Connaught and Mill Road cemeteries and the Thiepval Memorial. *Nigel Cave*

worst economic recessions. It was the final and largest memorial to Britain's missing. The structure is a sequence of massive stepped archways climbing to a final height of 150 feet. The bulk of the construction is brick but the lower piers are faced with portland stone upon which the names of the missing are engraved. It was unveiled on 31st July, 1932, by the Prince of Wales in the presence of the President of France.

Much false information is inadvertently circulated about this memorial. The memorial was not built on the site of the old village Chateau. The memorial does not record the names of all the soldiers who were killed during the 'Battle of the Somme'. In all there were approximately 125,000 men who were killed during the fighting in 1916, many of those from parts of the Empire, Australia, Canada, India, New Zealand and South Africa, but the majority coming from the United Kingdom. The Thiepval Memorial does however commemorate the UK and South African soldiers who were killed, but have no known grave, during the fighting in this area up to 20th March 1918. In total that is 72,085 men and of that number approximately ninety per cent are the names of men who died in the period July to November 1916, the First Battle of

A sequence of photographs which show the Thiepval memorial during the final stages of its construction.

the Somme. The memorial is testimony to the fact that many of these soldiers did not receive the dignity of a burial under a named headstone. This is simply explained. Many were obliterated by shellfire. Sometimes their bodies or fragments were not recovered until later battlefield clearances in late 1916 and early 1917 or after the war by which time all traces of identity had rotted or been lost. A significant number, up to one thousand, have since been identified. If you are searching for the memorial dealing with the missing after 20th March 1918, that is during the Second Battle of the Somme, you should consider visiting the Pozieres Memorial south-west of that village on the Albert to Bapaume road. It is also worth noting that there are separate memorials to the Empire missing at Villers-Bretonneux (Australia), Vimy Ridge (Canada), Neuve Chapelle (India), Beaumont Hamel (Newfoundland) and Longueval (New Zealand).

Understandably, in view of how much land had been donated by France for the establishment of the many cemeteries and memorials, Thiepval was chosen to record the joint nature of the Anglo-French offensive on the Somme in 1916. The words *Aux*

131

Armees Francaises et Britanniques L'Empire Britannique Reconnaissant are inscribed just below the summit of the memorial. There is also a joint cemetery in the memorial park just a few yards due west of the memorial. It contains the bodies of six hundred soldiers, equally divided between French and British troops, all found in the area in the months before the opening of the memorial.

The memorial stands upon the spur which runs south-westwards towards the site of the Leipzig Salient. The correct trench map reference for the car park entrance to the memorial is sheet 57 d S.E. 1&2 (parts of) R.31.b.4,9. The ground here is approximately 144 metres above sea level, the highest ground in the area being the Schwaben Redoubt at 153 metres and which rather precludes the view north-north-east past Grandcourt. At an early stage in the planning it had been thought that the memorial would straddle the Thiepval to Authuille road, rather after the style of the Menin Gate at Ypres. On 1st July 1916 Thiepval was attacked by men of 96 Brigade, the Salford Pals facing Thiepval directly and the Tyneside Commercials facing the site of the memorial from their positions in front of Thiepval Wood (Bois d'Authuille).

It is worth noting here the magnificent work of the Commonwealth War Graves Commission. The Thiepval Memorial is the largest of many hundreds of structures and cemeteries maintained by the commission. This work is always carried out with the meticulous attention to detail and reverence for which the Commission is noted. The staff of this organization have an unrivalled reputation for thoroughness and care. The Commission's staff are willing and able to help with requests to identify the grave or memorial which commemorates soldiers who died during the war. For obvious reasons that will be done freely for family antecedents but a charge may be levied if you request details on multiple names for research purposes. In every case it will speed an enquiry greatly if you can provide some pieces of background information such as a date of birth, date of death, military unit or service number.

The telephone number of the CWGC is 01628 34221. They are located at 2 Marlow Road, Maidenhead, Berks, SL6 7DX.

The Ulster Memorial Tower

The Ulster Memorial Tower is Northern Ireland's national war memorial. Although it has come to be associated in the public consciousness, because of its location near Thiepval, with the 36th (Ulster) Division it also commemorates the duty and sacrifice of all enlisted men from the six counties who served with many units during the Great War. Apart from the 36th (Ulster) Division there were also two other divisions raised on the island of Ireland. The 10th (Irish) Division was the first Irish unit to be raised as part of Kitchener's New Armies. It saw service at Gallipoli and in the Middle Eastern theatres of the war. The 16th (Irish) Division consisted of many Roman Catholics, from throughout the island and who had served with the Irish National Volunteers, as well as a number of Ulster Battalions and the 6th Connaught Rangers who numbered amongst their ranks 600 Ulstermen recruited in the main from Belfast. The 16th (Irish) Division is most closely linked with the fighting around Guillemont and Ginchy during the September of 1916. In June 1917 many units of the 36th and 16th Divisions were to find themselves fighting side by side in the same cause at the Battle of Messines Ridge and in August at the Battle of Frezenburg Ridge.

The Ulster Memorial Tower was built during 1921, becoming the first official memorial to be established along the Western Front. It was unveiled, on 21st November that year, by Field Marshal Sir Henry Wilson, the Chief of the Imperial General Staff who would later be assassinated by the IRA. The architecture of the tower is not however unique. It is a replica of Helen's Tower on the Clandeboye Estate in County Down between Belfast and Strangford Lough. This estate, which is home to the Marquesses of Dufferin and Ava, was the site of one of a number of camps employed to train the Ulster Division's men.

Unfortunately, for safety reasons, the top level of the tower is generally not open to the public today. However, in 1994 a substantial change was effected to the Ulster Tower which greatly enhances the visitor's appreciation of this locality. The Somme Association has opened a visitor's centre immediately behind the tower, housing exhibitions and audio-visual presentations. Car parking, refreshments, toilets and tourist information are also available. The centre is open Tuesday to Sunday but closed on Mondays and throughout December and January except by appointment. The tower can be contacted by telephone on (00 33) 22 74 87 14. Its address is La Tour d'Ulster, 80300 Thiepval, France. The tower is administered by the Northern Ireland Office but staffed by The Somme Association. The purpose of that association is to enhance the relationship between the two traditions in Northern Ireland by furthering research into and understanding of their common heritage and shared experience of the Great War. Close by the tower a small number of further memorials

The Ulster Tower today. From the top of the tower some remarkable views over the surrounding battlefields are possible. Unfortunately access to the top is denied to the public for safety reasons.

have been established. Within the grounds the most prominent is one commemorating the 36th Division's Victoria Cross winners. Just outside the gates stands the marble obelisk commemorating the men and women of the Orange Institution who have been killed in many fields of conflict.

The stone plaque which records the names of the nine men and officers who won the Victoria Cross whilst serving with the 36th Division. Outside the grounds is the Orange Institution obelisk.

July 1st, 1995. The Thiepval Road looking towards St Pierre Divion, and a lone khaki clad figure, a member of the Great War Society, looks across the scene of the attack made by the 36th (Ulster) Division 79 years ago.

The tower is located adjacent to the Thiepval Road running towards St. Pierre Divion in a stand of mature pine trees. Near to where the Mill Road leaves Thiepval Road was a small prominence in the German front lines known as the Pope's Nose (R.19.c.2,5). Approximately 500 yards to the north-east lay the German support position known as the Strassburg Lines. That important trench lay near to the old Divion Road which ran up the slope towards the north of Thiepval past the village's communal cemetery. Although the trenches around the tower's location were initially captured by the Ulstermen the bulk of the German front lines and support positions in this area were not captured until 13th November, four and a half months after the opening of the battle.

The 18th Division's Memorial — Thiepval

This requires no further explanation save to say that the location provides a magnificent panoramic view.

The 18th Division's memorial, past which can be seen the Connaught cemetery and the Ulster Tower.

The Salford Pals' Memorial, unveiled in the summer of 1995, eighty years after the arrival of the 32nd Division in this area.

The Salford Pals' Memorial — Authuille

In the final few hours before the 32nd Division's attacks upon Thiepval, on the morning of 1st July 1916, more than 2,000 men in three battalions raised from the dock-lands, textile works, factories and coal pits of Salford marched through Authuille as they assembled in readiness for that attack. Very few would survive the experience physically or mentally unscathed. In the previous months these men had made Aveluy Wood, the Ancre valley, Thiepval Wood, the Bluff and Black Horse shelters their home. The last known survivor of those distant events, Private Frank Holding of the 16th Lancashire Fusiliers — the 2nd Salford Pals, died in 1994. In the post war period the village of Authuille was adopted by the 'Urban District of Leyton', but little seems to have come of that association. More recently there has been a growth of interest in the local dimension of much of the history of the Great War. In particular this has centred round the recruitment of Pals units from many industrial cities and the four Salford Pals battalions are a moving example of this phenomena. During the early 1990s the Western Front Association in the Liverpool and Greater Manchester areas have been active in raising finance for a number of fitting monuments at Montauban and Mametz and the Salford Pals are now commemorated in the memorial which stands next to the village war memorial overlooking the main street of Authuille. It would be difficult to think of a more appropriate place.

The Mayor of Authuille, Monsieur Glavieux, and the author at the unveiling of the Salford Pals' memorial, 1st July 1995. The guard of honour was provided by members of the Great War Society.

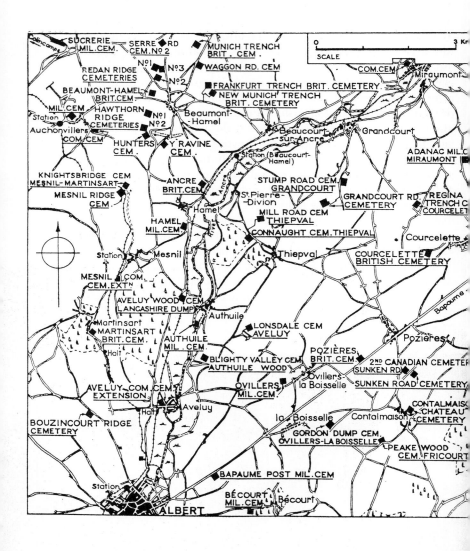

Map 18. The CWGC map which shows the location of the cemeteries within the Thiepval area.

Aveluy Communal Cemetery Extension

This can be reached within a few yards easy walk from the village centre. In many ways the cemetery here is an analogy for the entire British Army's experience around the village of Thiepval during the Great War. The cemetery was begun by French units and taken over by the British in July 1915. Field Ambulances operated here from August of that year through to November 1917. On 26-27th March 1918 the village and cemetery were captured by the Germans only to be retaken at the end of August after which just two more graves were dug. There are 613 graves of which only twenty-seven are unidentified. Apart from the many men who were killed or later died from wounds received during the fighting around Thiepval ridge, the cemetery shows the worldwide nature of the conflict, containing the graves of men from as far afield as South Africa, India, Australia, the UK, Brazil, Canada and Australia. Thirty French and eight German graves have been removed to other cemeteries.

The Aveluy Communal Cemetery Extension is laid across a gentle slope close by the village centre.

Authuille British Military Cemetery

The most lovely of the cemeteries in the Thiepval area. This is easily reached, on foot only, down the signposted path near to the church in the village. This is a genuine battlefield cemetery which contains 473 graves from throughout the 1915 – 1918 period. The cemetery was constructed on the reverse of a convex slope which gave protection from observed artillery and small arms fire, even though the cemetery was relatively close to the front lines. The bulk of these graves relate to the period between mid 1915 to December 1916 when the cemetery was used by fighting units and Field Ambulance units. During 1917 and 1918 the cemetery was used by Indian Labour Companies. The graves of two German prisoners, and all of the French military graves which surrounded the communal cemetery above, have been removed elsewhere. Since this cemetery was not enlarged by later clearances and concentrations there are only thirty-eight unnamed graves. Special memorials have been established to recall eighteen UK soldiers known or believed to be buried amongst that number. There are many graves of the men who served with the 36th and 32nd Divisions in front of Thiepval and the dates upon which German raids and bombardments caused heavy casualties during the first six months of 1916 are clearly identifiable in patterns running through these dates.

Aveluy Wood (Lancashire Dump) Cemetery

This can be reached on the D50 running north, through Aveluy Wood, from Aveluy in the direction of Hamel. The cemetery lies roughly 200 metres from the northern perimeter of the wood on the right hand side of the road, on the slope leading down to the Albert – Arras Railway. The construction of the cemetery followed a complex evolution. It was started in June 1916 and was used by fighting units and Field Ambulances until the German retirement of February 1917. The original graves are scattered almost haphazardly at the foot of the slope to the left of the Great Cross. In the spring of 1918 the German Army entered and occupied the wood but were evicted after severe fighting in August. In September the graves of men killed in the area between the April and September of 1918 were dug in Plot 1, Row H. After the Armistice Plots II and III were added, nearer to the cemetery entrance gate, to accommodate isolated graves from within Aveluy Wood. In 1923 Rows I to M of Plot 1 were added by concentrations from a wider area. There are 360 graves within this cemetery of which 175 are unidentified. Like Authuille, Aveluy Wood is another beautiful cemetery, especially in the evening sunshine.

Aveluy Wood Cemetery.

Blighty Valley Cemetery

This can be reached along the D151 south of Authuille. The path leading to the cemetery leads off to the left up the valley. The original graves face the Great Cross and contain the remains of men killed between July and November 1916. After this period the cemetery was not used until after the Armistice when 748 further graves were concentrated here from battlefields and small cemeteries to the east. The most important of those small cemeteries was Quarry Post, from where fifty graves, mostly of men belonging to the 12th (Eastern Division), came. These concentrations resulted in a cemetery within which a very high proportion of the men were killed during the fighting on and soon after 1st July 1916, mostly around the Leipzig Redoubt and along the Ovillers ridge. The cemetery contains 1,001 graves of which 532 are unknown. There are special memorial headstones to twenty-four UK soldiers known or believed to be buried amongst that number. There are also five other special headstones commemorating UK soldiers buried in Becourt German Cemetery, in the spring of 1918, whose graves could not be found on exhumation. Dug into the embankment on the north side of the cemetery were the Brigade headquarters which controlled the fighting in the Leipzig Redoubt and Authuille Wood areas during early July 1916.

The cemetery in Blighty Valley immediately after the war.
The same cemetery today.

Connaught Cemetery

Connaught Cemetery

This is a large cemetery whose size grew considerably in the post war period as a result of concentrations from smaller nearby burial grounds and battlefield clearance work. At the Armistice the cemetery contained 228 graves, all within Plot 1 except 10 further graves. It now contains 1,278 graves of which 642 are unnamed, 425 not even identified by their unit. Special memorials are erected to two UK soldiers believed to be buried amongst the unnamed graves, as well as five who were buried in Divion Road No. 2 but whose graves could not be found upon concentration. The work of concentration into Connaught eliminated many small burial grounds scattered around the battlefield in this area. Along with the concentrations into Mill Road Cemetery this work ensured that the Thiepval Memorial to he Missing would not be seen to be cluttered by nearby cemeteries. The principal cemeteries which were removed into Connaught were as follows:

Thiepval Village Cemetery on the summit of the ridge, west of la Grande Ferme, which contained 215 British soldier's graves.

Thiepval Valley Cemetery on the south-east side of Thiepval Wood which contained eleven British graves.

Quarry Palace Cemetery which was close to the River Ancre just north-east of St Pierre Divion and which contained twenty-three British graves from the period autumn 1916-1917.

St Pierre Divion Nos. 1 & 2 Cemeteries which were a little south-east of that hamlet which contained seventy British graves from the summer and autumn fighting of 1916.

The Small Connaught Cemetery which was opposite the present site and which contained fourty-one British soldiers who fell mainly on July 1st 1916 here.

Battery Valley Cemetery, Grandcourt. This contained fifty-six British graves from the period November-December 1916 and one from July 1917.

Paisley Hillside Cemetery. This was located on the south side of Thiepval Wood. Some graves were transferred to the Lonsdale Cemetery, the remainder here to Connaught. Originally Paisley Hillside contained thirty-two British graves from July and August 1916, mainly of men serving with the 49th (West Riding) Division.

Gordon Castle Cemetery which was located within Thiepval Wood. This contained thirty-three British graves from the July-September 1916 period of fighting, (again twenty-six of them men who served with the 49th Division), and the grave of one French soldier who fell in October 1914.

Bluff Cemetery, half a mile north of Authuille on the steep slope west of the junction between the D151 and the small road which leads to the west of Thiepval Wood alongside the Ancre. This originally contained forty-three British graves from the period July-September 1916.

Grandcourt Road Cemetery

This can be reached across the fields from the end of the Stump Road above Grandcourt. Leave Grandcourt on the D151 in the direction of Thiepval. At the first cross roads turn left onto Stump Road. Carry on past Stump Road British Military Cemetery and Grandcourt Road Cemetery is signposted on your right, towards the west, with splendid views to the north. Unfortunately the farmer

Grandcourt Road Cemetery.

here has seen fit to plough the path leading to this cemetery. The name Grandcourt Road is a complete misnomer in that the real Grandcourt Road was some distance to the east, leading towards Courcelette.

The small cemetery of Grandcourt Road contains 390 graves amongst which 108 are unidentified. A special memorial records the name of one soldier known to be buried amongst that number. The cemetery was constructed in the spring of 1917, after the German withdrawal, when the Ancre Battlefield was initially cleared. Many of the graves recall men who were killed during the late autumn fighting east of Schwaben Redoubt and around Stuff Redoubt.

Knightsbridge and Mesnil Ridge Cemeteries, Mesnil-Martinsart
These two interesting cemeteries can be reached by leaving Mesnil west on the D174. As you leave the village follow the CWGC sign pointing right along the lane leading north. The cemeteries are approximately one and a half kilometres distant. As you approach them Mesnil Ridge is on the left with Knightsbridge opposite.

Knightsbridge Cemetery.

Knightsbridge Cemetery
Knightsbridge cemetery has a link with the Thiepval fighting in that a number of men killed there are buried at the cemetery. The cemetery's name derives from a nearby communication trench. The site was used for burials during the period after the start of the Somme battles in 1916 through to the German withdrawal in February 1917, as well as during the period after the German

advance in March 1918 through to July 1918. After the armistice 112 other graves were added in rows G, H and J drawn from small battlefield burial sites from the area around Mesnil. There are 548 graves in the Knightsbridge cemetery of which 141 are unidentified.

Mesnil Ridge Cemetery.

Mesnil Ridge Cemetery

Mesnil Ridge cemetery is very different in character. This much more intimate cemetery was made by Field Ambulance and fighting units during a period of one year from August 1915 onwards. The cemetery contains ninety-five graves. Because it was not enlarged by later battlefield clearance the cemetery is unusual in that only one of the graves is unidentified. Many of the men came from the 29th and 36th (Ulster) Divisions and most of the graves recall men who died as a result of the raids and bombardments in this area during the spring and early summer of 1916.

Lonsdale Cemetery

This can be reached from the Authuille to Ovillers road which runs past the site of the Leipzig Redoubt. A narrow grass path leads across fields to the cemetery entrance. That entrance is a fine place from which to consider the events of 1st July in this area. The cemetery lies just to the north of Authuille Wood and is one of the larger burial grounds in this area. It contains 1,519 graves many of which have been concentrated here from four nearby small battlefield cemeteries. Those were Lonsdale Cemetery No. 2 which was sited 455 yards further east and which originally contained thirty-eight UK soldiers (thjirty-one of whom belonged to the 11th Borders), Nab Road Cemetery on the road

Lonsdale Cemetery.

running up Nab Valley which contained the graves of twenty-seven UK soldiers who fell during July, September and October 1916, as well as Paisley Avenue and Paisley Hillside cemeteries which were on the south side of Thiepval Wood.

The original part of Lonsdale cemetery, Plot 1, contained ninety-six graves almost all of which were those of officers and men belonging to the 1st Dorsets and 11th Borders (the Lonsdale Battalion). After the Armistice the cemetery was enlarged by the concentration of 1,425 further graves, almost all of which pertained to the fighting in 1916. Of the 1,519 graves, 815 are unidentified. This is due to the fact that most bodies were recovered as a result of post war battlefield clearances. There are also special memorials to twenty-two soldiers known or believed to be buried amongst that number.

Martinsart British Military Cemetery.

This can be reached easily from the road out of Martinsart village leading towards Aveluy. Just a few yards south of the village you will find the cemetery on your left above the road embankment with a crucifix to the right of the entrance. This cemetery has a unique atmosphere, being constructed of sandstone in an experiment relating to the wear characteristics of the stone. Most tragically the first grave in Plot 1, Row A is that of the fourteen men belonging to the 13th Royal Irish Rifles who were killed nearby, by a single German shell, on the 28th June, 1916. It was used as a front line cemetery until October 1916 and later in

September 1918. After the war it was enlarged by the concentration of 346 graves from the surrounding area. Sixteen German prisoners are buried within the cemetery and the unnamed graves number 156, special memorials commemorating six UK soldiers believed to be buried amongst that number.

Martinsart Cemetery.

Mesnil Communal Cemetery Extension
This can be found approximately half way between the village of Mesnil and Martinsart. It is located within yards of the western extremity of Aveluy Wood. The extension to the communal cemetery was begun in July 1916 and used again as a front line cemetery during 1918. After the war 141 graves from the Mesnil

Mesnil Communal Cemetery Extension.

Dressing Station Cemetery were brought here, along with 103 further graves from the battlefields of 1916 and 1918, north-east of Mesnil. The cemetery now contains the graves of 333 soldiers, of whom ninety-three are unnamed.

Mill Road Cemetery

This can be reached by a track which leads off the D73 Thiepval to Hamel road opposite the Connaught Cemetery. Along with Connaught Cemetery, Mill Road is one of the most frequently visited and well known of locations around Thiepval. It was originally known as Mill Road No. 2 Cemetery. It is unique within the area in that many of the headstones are laid flat in order to prevent the symmetry being disturbed by the constant subsidence of tunnels and dug-outs beneath the cemetery. Apart from the 260 graves in the original Plot 1, the cemetery was enlarged by the concentration of four smaller local battlefield cemeteries. These were Divion Road Cemetery No. 1, which was originally almost one mile south of St Pierre Divion on the road leading to the Ulster Tower and contained the bodies of twenty-nine men who fell in July and September 1916; the nearby Divion Road No. 3 Cemetery which contained the graves of a further forty-four men who fell in September and October 1916; Mill Road No. 1 Cemetery which was close to the present cemetery and St Pierre Divion Cemetery No. 2 which was constructed on the old Divion Road, which lay to the north of the present Mill Road Cemetery, and contained the graves of twenty-eight men who fell during September – October 1916.

Mill Road Cemetery.

151

Mill Road Cemetery.

There are 1,304 graves in this cemetery of which 815 are unidentified. Special memorials exist to three men believed to be buried here amongst this number. Other special memorials record the names of three men originally buried in Divion Road No. 1 whose graves were later destroyed by shellfire. There are a very significant number of men who served within the 36th (Ulster) Division who are buried within this cemetery. Post war battlefield concentrations and clearances also ensured that the remains of many men killed during the autumn fighting around Thiepval, Schwaben Redoubt and Stuff Redoubt would be brought here.

Stump Road Cemetery.

Stump Road Cemetery

Follow the directions as for Grandcourt Road Cemetery. Stump Road Cemetery is forty yards east of the Stump Road on your left as you rise up the slope. Within this small burial ground there are 263 graves, of which fifty are unnamed. Many of the graves recall men who served within the 18th Division and all are of men who fell during the period July 1916 to February 1917.

Executions by firing squad

Reference has been made within the text to three soldiers who were shot at dawn on conviction of desertion. These men are buried at two cemeteries which lie outside our area but which can be reached quickly. Private J. Crozier, 14218, 9th Royal Irish Rifles, is buried at the Sucrerie Military Cemetery near Colincamps. This is a fine cemetery which lies on the D 919 road between Mailly-Maillet and Serre. Take the D 73 road from Hamel past Newfoundland Park to Auchonvillers. Leave that village in the direction of Beaumont Hamel but then turn left into the D 174 which will take you to the Serre Road where you will see the Sucrerie Cemetery across the road to your left.

Riflemen J. McCracken, 13211, and J. Templeton, 890, both of the 15th Royal Irish Rifles, are buried at Mailly-Maillet Communal Cemetery Extension. This can be found by continuing south-westwards along the D 919 from the Sucrerie into Mailly-Maillet. In the village centre turn right in the direction of Colincamps. Just outside Mailly-Maillet fork left and you will find the communal cemetery with its military extension.

Chapter Seven
FOUR TOURS OF THE AREA

This section of the guide provides a series of four tours. The first of these is a general tour, too long to undertake except by car or coach, designed to make you familiar with the main features and sights found within the area. The three tours which follow can all be easily conducted on foot or mountain cycle and will allow you to develop a more detailed understanding of particular locations.

March 1918 — Bouzincourt. Prisoners taken during the German offensive known as 'Operation Michael' during which the speed of movement sometimes left whole units isolated behind British lines.

Tour one. A general tour of the area to familiarize yourself with the main features around Thiepval.

This is suitable for all cars and most coaches. If you stop at all the suggested locations this may well take three hours to complete. I suggest that you make use of the relevant IGN maps. The Green series 1:100,000 Laon — Arras sheet will suffice, but more detail can be gleaned by making use of the Blue series 1:25,000 sheets, the three most useful being 2407 east and west with 2408 west to cover the Albert and Aveluy areas. However, the map below will help if you have been unable to obtain the IGN sheets.

A suitable starting point is the town of Albert. Leave on the Amiens road, the D929, but turn right two hundred and fifty metres from the town centre onto the D938 heading north-west in the direction of Bouzincourt. West of Bouzincourt are the many billet villages familiar to the troops who served here. During 1915 and 1916 Bouzincourt lay some miles behind the British lines and

Map 19. Route map for the tour of the Albert - Thiepval area.

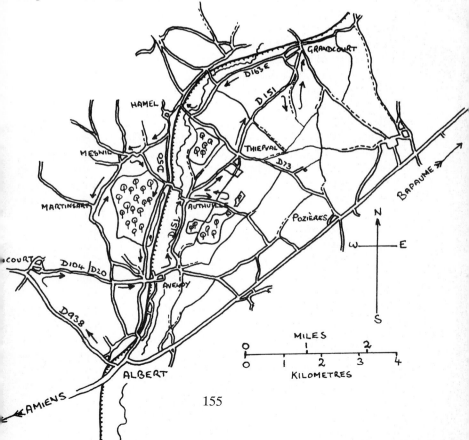

155

housed many divisional command and communication posts as well as a main dressing station and the major medical evacuation facilities which were prepared prior to the Big Push of July 1916. There is a communal cemetery and extension here, the village being used as a Field Ambulance Station from early 1916 to February 1917. However, the views from Bouzincourt are restricted by the terrain and a far better prospect can be obtained by turning right and leaving the village on the D20 Bouzincourt to Aveluy road. One and a half kilometres along that road lies an area of higher ground with fine views in the direction of Thiepval and over Albert. It was along this dusty track, and on a little north running out of Martinsart, that many of the casualties from 1st July's fighting at Thiepval were evacuated. Bouzincourt Ridge British Military Cemetery can be reached along the sunken lane to the right which leaves the Bouzincourt road here. This sunken lane is not passable by car except with great caution in mid summer. A pleasant walk of eight hundred metres takes you to the cemetery entrance gateway, whose design mirrors that of the Thiepval memorial arch which can be seen clearly in the distance. This cemetery contains 708 graves.

Continue eastwards and downhill towards Aveluy, still along the D20. During 1916 the village of Aveluy was in British hands, only to be captured by the Germans, in late March 1918. Aveluy village contains a British military cemetery built as an extension to the village's communal graveyard. The cemetery here was used by the British Army from August 1915 until March 1917. It was constructed next to a Field Ambulance and contains the graves of many men who died of wounds there. The cemetery can be reached by crossing over the cross roads at the D50, and thence over the railway bridge before entering the wide junction keeping to the left in the direction of Authuille. Turn sharp left just beyond this junction and the cemetery is one hundred and fifty metres along the lane, on your left. Return to the D20 and continue eastwards towards Authuille. As you leave Aveluy the road slopes down towards the Ancre. The river has been canalized here. On your left was one of the iron bridges constructed by the British engineers to carry traffic towards Thiepval and which was only demolished during 1995. At the 'T' junction three hundred metres away is the left turn towards Authuille. This is the notorious Crucifix Corner which was an important forward dump and water cart filling point from which hundreds of wiring parties were sent up to reinforce the British defences on the Ovillers ridge and in front of the Leipzig Redoubt. Today the corner is marked by a

The road out of Aveluy towards Crucifix Corner.

vehicle breaker's yard within the quarry behind the crucifix. In 1916 the quarry housed many shelters in dugouts under the east face of the chalk walls. Above the quarry were an important series of trenches known as the Bridgehead Defences. From the quarry an important trench tramway ran northwards alongside the east side of the Authuille Road.

Turn left at Crucifix Corner, along the D151 in the direction of Authuille. Cut into the roadside one hundred metres on your right are a series on gun pits used by artillery units during the bombardment of Thiepval and nearby locations during the last week of June 1916. The right hand side of the road was the location of the trench tramway. Soon, as the road rounds a spur of higher ground, you will see a valley to your right. This is Blighty Valley, along which a well maintained grass path leads to the British Cemetery which contains over 1,000 graves, almost half of which contain casualties from the 1st July's fighting. Behind the cemetery is the embankment within which the dugouts housing 14 and 97 Brigade HQs were established prior to the 1st July attacks across Leipzig Redoubt. Running along the valley floor the tramway then rose into the woods to a loading platform in the middle of the woodland area.

Above Blighty Valley Cemetery lies Authuille Wood (*Bois de la Haie*) which is the subject of a separate walking tour. If you prefer you can delay your visit to Blighty Valley until you choose to walk the Authuille Wood tour.

Return to the road and continue north along the D151, running parallel to the River Ancre. On your left, as the road rises slightly on the approach to Authuille, is the village communal cemetery. In 1915 many French soldiers had been buried here but those remains have since been removed to the large French National Cemetery on the D938 Peronne Road outside the town of Albert, to where all the small French battlefield cemeteries in this area were concentrated. The slopes behind Authuille's communal cemetery, above the River Ancre, were known as Black Horse shelters, roughly one hundred and fifty metres south of the village. Because of the convex nature of the slope they were generally free from small arms and artillery fire. The Black Horse road ran down through Aveluy Wood and across the Ancre marshes, thence over the causeway/bridge due west of the village cemetery. It was within the Black Horse shelters that many men of 14 Brigade took refuge before their march south and the abortive attempt to cross Leipzig Redoubt on the morning of 1st July, 1916.

The distinctive village church at Authuille.

The Authuille village war memorial and the site of the Salford Pals memorial, which stand looking down the main street of Authuille village, a scene which all of the men commemorated by the memorial would still recognize were they to see it today.

Enter the village of Authuille and drive past the distinctive village church. In front of you, in the triangle of the grassy embankment above the junction, are two memorials. The longest standing is the village war memorial which includes the name of Boromee Vaquette, the first Frenchman from the village to be killed here, as well as others whose descendants still live and work within the village. In a privileged position beside this is the recently established Salford Pals memorial. This records the close links with the village which the three Salford Pals Battalions, the 15th, 16th and 19th Lancashire Fusiliers, established throughout the first six months of 1916.

Take the sharp right turn up the slope opposite the village and Salford Pals' memorials in the direction of the Lonsdale Cemetery. This road is not really suitable for large coaches in that turning round to return is not easy, although cars and mini-buses will find quite satisfactory turning points. At the summit, to your left can be seen the Leipzig Salient and the Granatloch amongst the prominent group of trees. A little past the summit is the Lonsdale Cemetery near to which a number of British front line trenches can still be seen with care. This area will be dealt with in detail during the Authuille Wood area tour. Turn round and return to

Authuille along the same road, at the foot of which turn right onto the D151 again. Keep to the right at the fork outside Authuille.

You are now driving along the Authuille to Thiepval road.[1] On your left is Thiepval Wood, or Bois d'Authuille on your IGN map. This was the most important assembly point prior to the British attack on Thiepval on 1st July. Just to the left of Thiepval Wood can be seen Caterpillar Copse, either side of which ran two important communication trenches, Paisley Avenue on the north and Hamilton Avenue on the south. On your right, due east of Caterpillar Copse, lies the Thiepval Memorial to the Missing. As you pass the boundary fence of the Memorial and approach the church you will see a large farm on the left of the road, this is the site of the pre-war chateau. Many of today's visitors are under the impression, falsely, that the Memorial was built upon the site of that original chateau.

Thiepval Village church.

The cross roads next to Thiepval church is a fine vantage point. The buildings shown on trench and pre-1914 maps to the north-west of the church have been obliterated, leaving an uninterrupted view today. Look down the Thiepval road towards Thiepval Wood. The land to the left of the Thiepval road is the old chateau's gardens, within which a circular driveway once provided pleasant walks and an opportunity for quiet conversation. By late 1915 part of the British front line was located on this driveway with Thiepval Points North and South as small salients jutting towards the north and south of the chateau's buildings. At the bottom of those gardens Hammerhead Sap ran along the foot of the chateau's property, jutting out into No Man's Land parallel to the lane which once lay in the valley in front of Thiepval Wood. During 1916, in the gardens, two small stands of trees provided a landmark. On the German front line lay Diamond Wood, two hundred metres west of the chateau. In No Man's Land, one hundred metres forward of the British lines, lay Oblong Wood, to which a sap had been constructed from the British front line at the foot of the gardens.

Just to the left of the Thiepval road, eight hundred metres distant from the church and adjacent to Thiepval Wood, you can see Connaught Cemetery. Connaught marks the British front line positions facing Schwaben Redoubt. It was from this north-eastern face of Thiepval Wood that the Ulstermen debouched on the morning of 1st July. On the right of the road, immediately opposite Connaught, a path leads to Mill Road Cemetery, which is situated on the German forward lines just west of Schwaben Redoubt. Beyond both cemeteries lies the Ulster Tower which is built on the German front line above the slope running down to the Ancre, between St Pierre Divion and Hamel. The Thiepval Wood area is also the subject of a separate walking tour.

Running in an easterly direction from the church is the D73 leading to Pozieres. Mouquet farm can easily be reached from this road.

You can now move on towards Schwaben Redoubt by driving north out of Thiepval along the D151. Four hundred metres along the road out of the village is the communal cemetery. Keep right here and continue slightly uphill until you reach *la Grande Ferme* in another six hundred metres. This cluster of buildings is the site of *Feste Schwaben*, the highest point in the vicinity of Thiepval and the most imposingly fortified of the redoubts along the German front in this sector. Thiepval and the Schwaben Redoubt fell to the 18th Division during September and October 1916. Continue along the D151 past *la Grande Ferme* where you can see Battery

The 18th Division's memorial obelisk which stands just outside the park surrounding Edwin Lutyen's Memorial to the Missing. Apart from being a fine location from which to consider the massive memorial this spot also provides a fine view across the scene of the Tyneside Commercials and Salford Pals attacks on 1st July 1916.

Valley on your left (Vallee Caronnesse on your IGN map). Stop at the cross roads on the spur above Grandcourt (R.15.a.8.6. on your trench map). This is the eastern limit of this guide and on your right is the Stump Road, which is not suitable for coaches, leading up to *Feste Staufen* and *Feste Zollern*. Because those areas are isolated you may wish to explore them in detail now. More detailed directions appear within Tour Four which deals with Thiepval Village and the German rear defences.

After returning to the D151 from Stump Road turn right and drive down the slope into Grandcourt. Turn left and then left again to take the D4151 (marked D163E on IGN 1:25,000 maps) travelling west in the direction of St Pierre Divion. Ignore the right turn marked for Beaucourt and head straight on to St Pierre Divion's few buildings. During November of 1916 this area was the scene of the most hideous fighting within the valley of the Ancre. The onset of wet weather and the inability of the marshes to drain the area meant that troops were forced to fight and endure in the most unspeakably horrible conditions. Continue along the road through St Pierre Divion, with its maze of subterranean defences which were entered through the huge embankment to your left, until the junction with the D73 Thiepval road. Turn right and cross the Ancre and then the level crossing, beyond which you should turn left onto the D50. This will take you to Hamel. This was on the left of the 36th Division's lines. From the Mesnil Ridge, above Hamel, three important communication trenches ran down into Hamel. The most northerly was Esau Alley, coming down from Fort Jackson (Q.16.d,0,0), then Charles Avenue and lastly Jacob's Ladder, a particularly dangerous trench in that it was overlooked and enfiladed by fire from Schwaben and above Beaucourt. Staying on the D50 pass through the village of Hamel beyond which, just after the British Military Cemetery, you should take the right fork towards Mesnil along the C7. As you drive up the slope you are moving parallel to Jacob's Ladder, which ran two hundred yards to the right of the road as you proceed uphill. As you enter Mesnil you will come to the D174. A right turn here will be of special interest for those people following the story of the 36th Division's Ulstermen for whom it is worth noting that north of Mesnil, halfway to Auchonvillers along a track not accessible to coaches, lies Mesnil Ridge Military Cemetery. This cemetery contains the graves of many soldiers from the 36th Division killed during the period from their arrival in late 1915 through to July 916.

From Mesnil you should also make a small diversion to the village of Martinsart, one mile to the south west along the C7. Martinsart was the scene of the disaster which befell the 13th Royal Irish Rifles two days before the opening of the Somme offensive when one platoon of the battalion was devastated by the horrific effects of a single shell. Martinsart was important to the Ulsters as the origin of the tramway which maintained supplies to their Thiepval positions. It was also, quite extraordinarily in view of the size of the village, the permanent billet for five battalions of Ulstermen! During the final week long bombardment these five battalions were sent further back to Varennes, Leavillers, Hedauville and Forceville in order to avoid the expected German bombardment of Martinsart. In fact no substantial bombardment fell upon Martinsart until after the start of the Ulsters' attack. Just south of Martinsart, on the D129 heading towards Aveluy, you will be able to find Martinsart's military cemetery from where, due east, you can obtain good views towards Aveluy Wood. The fourteen men killed by that fateful shell are buried within the first graves dug within the cemetery. Now return to Mesnil.

Pass through the village and continue towards Mesnil's eccentric chateau, in a south-easterly direction, downhill along the D174 towards Authuille. Here, in front of the Chateau but on the left side of the road, you can stand at the site of 'Brock's Benefit' from which Brigadier General H.J. Brock of the 36th Division was able to monitor the effect of his artillery on the German's Thiepval defences opposite. Whilst you are at Brock's Benefit, looking down the D174, take note that on your right, behind the chateau, is Aveluy Wood. To your left, across the valley of the Ancre in the direction of the Thiepval memorial, is Thiepval Wood. In a line directly between Mesnil and Thiepval Wood lay the *Passerelle de Magenta*, across which were constructed two important causeways, north and south, each capable of carrying infantry in fours and 18 pounder gun limbers with their teams. Thiepval Wood provided cover for two branches of the trench tramway which was constructed during the early summer of 1916. One branch ran along the east face of the wood and served the requirements of the 36th Division there. The other branch ran along the southern edge of Thiepval Wood, between Paisley Avenue trench and Caterpillar Copse, and served the 32nd Division. At the foot of the slope turn right onto the D50 in the direction of Albert. After one hundred metres you will see Aveluy (Lancashire Dump) Cemetery on your left. This dates from mid summer 1916 and was used by units and Field Ambulances until early 1917 and later during 1918. Here, within the confines of the woodland, you can easily visualize the vital cover afforded by the trees. It was possible to assemble a division of troops within the woods without their being seen from the Thiepval ridge. The wood was therefore crucial in the processes of supplying the munitions and material needed by British units operating in the Thiepval sector. To help in this task the trench tramway had been built which originated in the valley between Aveluy Wood and Martinsart village, just below the military cemetery on the D129, and terminated in Thiepval Wood. The tramway rose from its start near Martinsart (54.d.S.E.4. W.4.a.0,0) through the southern end of Aveluy Wood and then ran alongside the Albert to Hamel road to a siding next to Lancashire Dump. From here the tramway ran east through a tunnel built under the main railway track and on towards the Ancre (which it crossed at the site of the present day river bridge at the Hotel des Pecheurs). As you drive back along the D50 through Aveluy Wood, towards Albert, you will be able to see glimpses of the view over the Ancre valley to your left. Below the road lies the main line railway cutting. Between that railway and the road are a vast network of trenches, many of which were constructed during 1918. You should be aware that this part of the wood is oft frequented by hunters who use traps and shotguns in pursuit of their Sunday dinner. Make sure you don't end up on their plate beside the quail and venison!

From here, in Aveluy Wood, it is just five minutes by car back into Albert by which time you should have a clear mental picture of the Thiepval area.

Tour Two. Authuille village and Authuille Wood area (Bois de la Haie).

This tour can only be undertaken on foot or with the aid of a mountain cycle. It is absolutely essential that you take the greatest care when entering any woodland. The wood is marked on the IGN 1:25,000 map (2408 west) as containing hunting lodges, so be warned!

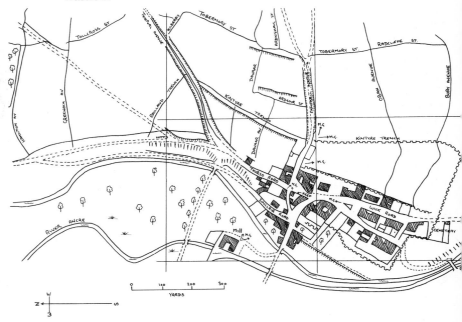

Map 20. Authuille village in the spring of 1916.

This wood is one of the most fascinating locations which can be found along the entire western front. The tour will focus on the attacks made by 97 and 14 Brigades on the morning of 1st July 1916. There are ample places to park in the village of Authuille from whence you can walk south along the D151. Before you go too far I suggest this is an opportune moment to visit the Authuille Military Cemetery. After passing the village church in the direction of Aveluy turn right and follow the farm road and path down to Authuille Military Cemetery. This is built on the northern end of the slopes of Black Horse Shelters and is one of the most intimate and beautiful of all the British Somme cemeteries. Charles Douie's words are especially eloquent in this location. In the spring of

166

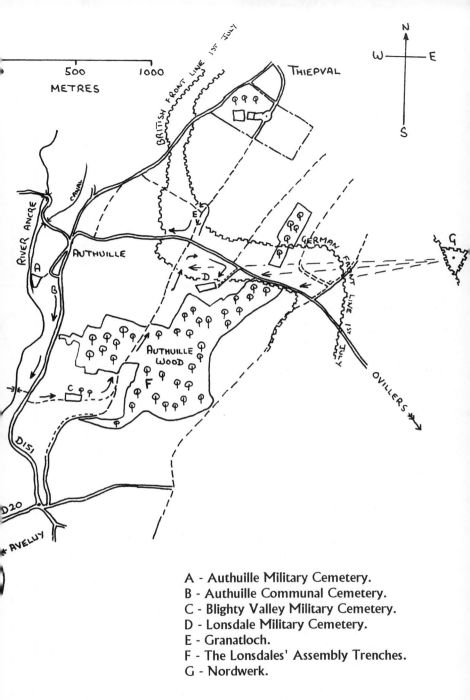

A - Authuille Military Cemetery.
B - Authuille Communal Cemetery.
C - Blighty Valley Military Cemetery.
D - Lonsdale Military Cemetery.
E - Granatloch.
F - The Lonsdales' Assembly Trenches.
G - Nordwerk.

Map 21. The Authuille Wood area (Bois de la Haie) tour.

167

1916 he stood beside you here on the banks of the Ancre, whilst serving with the 1st Dorsets. He was witness to a burial and his words are a timeless reflection of the feelings of soldiers towards their fallen comrades.

'On the edge of the bank, and just beyond the South Barricade of Authuille village, lay the French cemetery where the dead of the first few months of the war lay beside the dead of centuries of peace. The small cemetery had proved inadequate within a short time, and the graves lay outside and around it. Now there was a new and already large cemetery below. One evening I stood there looking over the broad marshes of the Ancre and the great mass of Aveluy Wood beyond. There was a lull in the firing, and everything was still. The sun was setting; perhaps the majesty of Nature had stayed for one moment the hand of the Angel of Death. The river and marshes were a sea of gold, and the trees of the wood were tinged with fire. To the south were the square tower of Aveluy Church and the great trees surrounding the crucifix at the junction of the roads, known as Crucifix Corner. Shadows were lengthening in the woods and on the marshes. A cool evening breeze blew gently through the graves of our dead.

'Before me lay men of many nations in their long sleep. The names inscribed on the dark crosses of the French were full of music; they were men of the Breton Corps, sons of Morbihan and Finisterre. Apart lay the grave of a man killed in the first month of the war, when Uhlan patrols came into contact with small bodies of British and French detached from their regiments. Nearby were the dead of the first autumn slain in the great fight for the ridge. Beyond were the men who had died in the long and monotonous days of trench warfare, which for eighteen months had taken, day by day, its toll of human life, of the flower of two nations...

'In the far corner a padre stood reading the burial service, while a group of men with bowed and uncovered heads stood round a new grave. Here indeed death held nothing of indignity, and all was simple and sincere. It was a scene of quiet grandeur. No king could dream of a more splendid resting-place, here above the marshes in the glory of the evening.

'The sun set; twilight drew on. The evening star glimmered above the far horizon. The marshes were grey, and a mist rose from the water. Dark shadows enveloped the woods.

There was a roar as a shrapnel shell burst, and the smoke hung like a pall over the ground where once Authuille had stood, now a ruin where death stalked night and day. A machine gun opened fire in the trenches, and the crash of bombs re-echoed through the trees. The weary night watches had begun. The wind rose. The Angel of Death was abroad, and in the wind I could hear the beating of his wings.'[2]

In that spring of 1916 Black Horse shelters provided the site of battalion HQs who were operating as Brigade Reserve in the Thiepval sector. Here, in the adjacent military cemetery which Douie so movingly described, are buried many of the 32nd Division's casualties incurred from the raids and random shellfire of the early months of 1916. One particularly poignant grave is that of Willie McBride whom those of you with folk songs in your hearts will recognize as the object of one small simple 1960's anthem which questioned the personal costs of the war.[3]

Well, how do you do, Private William McBride?
Do you mind if I sit here, down by your graveside?
And rest for a while in the warm summer sun,
I've been walking all day, and I'm nearly done.
And I see by your gravestone you were only nineteen
When you joined the Glorious Fallen in nineteen sixteen,
Well I hope you died quick, and I hope you died clean,
Or Willie McBride, was it slow and obscene?

> **Chorus:**
> Did they beat the drum slowly?
> Did they play the pipes lowly?
> Did the rifles fire to'er ye
> As they lowered you down?
> Did the bugles sing the 'Last Post' in chorus?
> Did the pipes play 'The Flowers of the Forest'?

And did you leave a wife or a sweetheart behind?
In some faithful heart is your memory enshrined?
And although you died back in nineteen sixteen,
To that loyal heart, are you always nineteen?
Or are you just a stranger without even a name,
Forever enshrined behind some glass pane,
In an old photograph, torn and tattered and stained,
And fading to yellow in a brown leather frame?

Chorus:
Well, the Sun, it shines down on these green fields of France,
The warm wind blows gently and the red poppies dance,
The trenches are vanished and under the plough,
No gas and barbed wire, no guns firing now,
But here, in this graveyard, it's still No Man's Land,
And countless white crosses in mute witness stand,
To man's blind indifference to his fellow man,
And a whole generation who were butchered and damned.

Chorus:
And I can't help but wonder, now, Willie McBride,
Do all those who lie here know why they died?
Did you really believe them when they told you the cause?
Did you really believe that this war would end wars?
But the suffering, the dying, it was all done in vain,
For Willie McBride, it's happened again,
And again, and again, and again, and again.

Leave the Authuille Military cemetery and continue along the D151 towards Aveluy. Behind the communal cemetery, on your right, are the Black Horse shelters, within which the men who would attack the German second line positions at Mouquet Farm were shaving at 5.30 am, on 1st July 1916. From here, at 7.10 am, that morning, the column which included the 1st Dorsets, 14 Brigade Trench Mortar Battery, four Stokes guns, the 19th Lancashire Fusiliers and a half section of 206 Company of the Royal Engineers were paraded and set out in columns of fours. The previous night these men had marched from billets at Senlis. As you reach the throat of Blighty Valley glance west across the Ancre. The small bridge is on the site of 'Jardine Bridge', named after 97 Brigade's Commanding Officer, where the column turned left away from the bed of the Ancre and marched towards Authuille Wood. As they marched in, grim faced, the wild cacophony of the final hurricane bombardment directed at Thiepval and the Leipzig Redoubt positions above was being played out.

Aerial photograph showing Authuille village and Authuille Wood before the shellfire and battles of 1916 destroyed the agricultural symmetry of the area. The crop patterns are still clearly visible and you should have little difficulty in relating this photograph to many of the maps which cover the same area.

Walk along to the cemetery and note the wooded embankment to the rear. On the morning of 1st July 1916, just south from here, one and a half battalions of 14 Brigade, the 15th HLI and two companies of the 2nd Manchesters, were in shelters at Crucifix Corner quarry also awaiting orders to move up to attack the Mouquet Farm and Goat Redoubt area. Continue past the cemetery skirting the field and keeping to the wooded area, for roughly one hundred metres. Towards the east end of that copse were the battle HQs for 97 and 14 Brigades on the morning of 1st July. The mounds of those deep dugouts are still clearly visible today. A little way further on join the track which runs north, up the slope, and into Authuille Wood. Before walking up that rise a glance to your right reveals the broad floor of the valley which housed many field gun batteries throughout the summer of 1916. During the final week's bombardment the guns were almost wheel to wheel here and were being served by the trench tramway whose tracks ran beside the cemetery and into the southern portion of the wood. As you walk up the slope, about twenty yards before the gate at the top of the rise, look to your right. One hundred metres inside that wood on your right were the assembly positions for the 11th Borders, the Lonsdales, as they awaited their terrible fate. It was along this same track on which you are standing that the 1st Dorsets and the 19th Lancashire Fusiliers (3rd Salford Pals) were brought up to their assembly positions, north-east of the gate alongside Dumbarton Track (at X.1.c.3,7). The start of Dumbarton track is within yards on the right as you enter the wood. However, its further course is not easy to follow today and you should walk straight ahead in a northerly direction.

Walk through the wood continuing up the slope along the main track. To the left and right are many shell holes, gun pits and shallow assembly trenches. There were dumps here for 2,000,000 rounds of small arms ammunition as well as 4,800 trench mortar rounds and 22,000 grenades. In two hundred metres, as you leave the wood, you are approaching Birtle Post from where the Lonsdales debouched and were slaughtered, many never even making the British front line! On the perimeter of the wood on your right are numerous trenches, but do not be deceived, the British front line is 500 metres further along the track, a position which could be reached more safely along two communication trenches in the summer of 1916. That to the west of the track was Kersall Street leading into Chowbent Street. To the east was Chequerbent Street. In the rush to get forward these trenches were not used by the 11th Borders, 1st Dorsets and 19th Lancashire

Fusiliers and consequently many of these battalions' men were cut down even before they reached the British front line. Although it is certain that Chequerbent and Chowbent were registered by the German artillery the non-use of these relatively safe havens can only be explained by their being overcrowded with casualties from the initial 7.30 am, assault. The 19th Lancashire Fusiliers 'Report on Operations' describes this over-ground rush in the following terms:

> 'owing to the severe casualties (11th Borders and 1st Dorsets) on leaving the wood, the OC RIGHT COLUMN brought up two trench mortars to point X.1.c.35,75 and also established two Lewis Guns and under cover of the fire of these guns the advance was continued. The open space in front of point X.1.c.35,75 was covered by squads in rushes of 30 to 40 yards — the men taking cover in shell craters. 'A' 'B' and half of 'C' companies then crossed the open space between point X.1.c.35,75 and our front line trench, heavy enfilade fire being experienced the whole way across, causing many casualties.'[4]

Almost all of those soldiers that did cross their own front line and then went on into No Man's Land were there broken by the enfilade machine gun fire coming from the Nordwerk, fifteen hundred metres to the east.

As you continue along the track and approach the prominent clump of poplar trees which ring the Granatloch you are standing in No Man's Land in front of the Leipzig Redoubt. It was here that Boromee Vaquette was driving his stakes into the ground to enclose his grazing cattle when he was mistakenly shot on the 27th September 1914. Before entering the Leipzig Redoubt area turn right towards the northern end of Blighty Valley in the direction of Ovillers. The junction with the 8th Division, the left division of III Corps, was 600 metres east of the cross roads here in No Man's Land. The bulk of the British lines from the track, south of the cross roads, to the junction with the 8th Division was held by the two remaining companies of the 2nd Manchesters and, in order to simplify the coordination of the units involved, no attack was launched from these trenches. The British front line here, in front of the Lonsdale Cemetery, was known as Boggart Hole Clough (located around X.1.a.5,4). The communication trenches leading to it were named after various Lancashire and Liverpudlian connections, Bury Avenue, Lime Street, Aintree Street, Mersey Street and others. One of the most important of these communication trenches, Tithebarn, is still clearly visible amongst the line of trees to the left of the path leading along to the Lonsdale Cemetery. If possible you can stroll across the field to the tip of the wood, past Tithebarn Street, where a considerable area of British front line, support and communication trenches lies undisturbed. During the initial attack here the Lonsdale battalion had suffered four hundred and ninety casualties amongst its men, as well as twenty-five officer casualties. The Lonsdale's cemetery is therefore a particularly moving location. The battalion, the 11th Borders, had been raised from the communities in Cumberland and Westmoreland by the Earl of Lonsdale and trained under the direction of its Commanding Officer, Lieutenant Colonel P.W. Machell. Machell became one of his battalion's many fatal casualties that fateful morning and is buried at Warloy-Baillon, in the 32nd Division's billet area east of Bouzincourt. The Lonsdale cemetery is the burial place of many men who attacked the Leipzig Redoubt on 1st July and is especially notable in that it contains the grave of Sgt James Turnbull, 15888, of the 17th Highland Light Infantry. A significant number of graves from the Thiepval Wood area have also been concentrated here.

Just yards from the Lonsdale cemetery, within Tithebarn communication trench, a great expanse of the British front line system can be seen.

Now return to the cross roads next to Leipzig Salient.

These cross roads, just south of the Granatloch, are a good place to gather your thoughts. Look along the road running west down to Authuille. The British front line was roughly seventy yards in that direction, a prominent position known as 'The Naze'. The British line then swung round in a roughly semicircular curve, above Authuille Wood, towards Boggart Hole Clough. By and large No Man's Land was one hundred and fifty metres wide in this area, but at the site of the Naze it was only eighty metres wide, a factor which gave enormous aid to the 17th HLI in their initially successful dash across here at 7.30 am on 1st July. The western face of the Leipzig Salient and Redoubt had been attacked by 97 Brigade, the 17th HLI making their lodgement in the south-western end of the redoubt. Spanning No Man's Land here was Sanda Sap which, late on 1st July, facilitated communication with the men who entered the Granatloch (Authuille quarry) near the tip of the Leipzig Redoubt. A second sap had been constructed 150 metres further north and connected the 16th HLI's positions with the Granatloch. Almost all of the 16th HLI's attack was unsuccessful, apart from some men of B company who attacked next to the 17th HLI's men. Small numbers of the 17th HLI did reach the *Hindenburg Stellung* during the initial assault, but were repulsed by the concentration of machine gun fire emanating from the *Wundt-Werk*. The main evacuation trench for the many British casualties incurred during this action was known as Oban Trench which ran due west, parallel to the Authuille road but 100 metres to its south. If you stand at The Naze and look along a line running to the eastern-most tip of Thiepval Wood (R.25.a. central) you are looking straight down the British 32nd Division's front lines facing Thiepval. Apart from the two HLI battalions (in the 97th Brigade) the other units which attacked along that line on 1st July at 7.30 am, were the 16th Northumberland Fusiliers and the 15th Lancashire Fusiliers (96 Brigade).

Of course the 96 Brigade's assault was a disaster. But here at the Granatloch the 17th HLI had effected the most northerly permanent bite into the German positions. Initially they were joined by small numbers from the 16th HLI, and later by some men of the 11th Borders and finally from 14 Brigade. However, despite determined attempts to advance over the top and by bombing along north and east of their positions these men were contained within the overcrowded and deadly confines of the maze of trenches within and above the quarry, which is today ringed with trees in an otherwise open area of fields. The reason for their

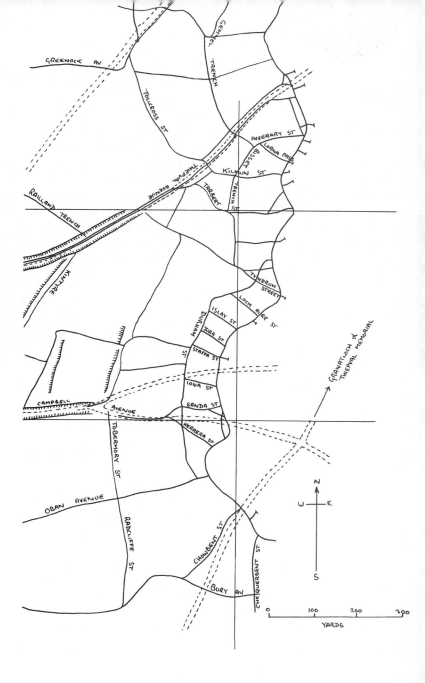

Map 22. The cross roads at the Granatloch with the named British trenches in this area running north in front of Thiepval village, spring 1916.

176

The ring of poplar trees which surrounds the Granatloch.

inability to progress is clear. A short walk into the quarry will provide fine views towards the Thiepval memorial. One hundred metres north-east of the quarry is the *Hindenburg Stellung*, and thence the succession of further wired fire trenches running back to the *Wundt-Werk*, five hundred metres north-east on the *Hohenzollern Stellung* and slightly on the reverse slope away from incoming British artillery fire from the west. From these positions a series of unremitting German counter attacks were thrown at the mixed bag of soldiers clinging desperately to their toe hold in the Leipzig Redoubt. Foremost amongst that stout band was Sergeant James Turnbull, of the 17th HLI, whose devotion to duty would win him the Victoria Cross and who was killed during his resolute defence of this position. By that evening the quarry was literally covered in a carpet of corpses, as was the field to the south where three battalions had been massacred within a couple of acres of bloodied land.

You can return to Authuille by following the road west, downhill, back to the D151. One hundred metres before that road you will cross the main village defences, known as the Kintyre Trenches, which ringed the north, east and south of Authuille.

This walk can best be started from Authuille village. Proceed north along the D151 in the direction of Thiepval past the Tree of Liberty on your left. Fifty metres beyond that tree you can look to the left down the embankment and over one of the vital causeways and Yatman Bridge which provided access for the troops across the waterlogged marshes here. Here, just outside the village, take the left fork and follow the contours in a northerly direction for 200 metres. On your left are wooded slopes leading down to the Ancre which contain many dugouts, including that housing 96 Brigade's headquarters on the morning of 1st July. This area was known to the Tommies as 'The Bluff'. On your right is the track which leads in a north-easterly direction, past the south-east face of Thiepval Wood. Avoid that track since it will provide our return route. This minor junction was the northern perimeter of the Authuille defences, the British second position, and the road was here crossed by a fire trench known as Railland Street which ran in a south-westerly direction up to the D151 where the line, known as the Kintyre trench, turned south and back towards a position above Authuille along the embankment which you can see.

Carry on for a further 600 metres, in a northerly direction and slightly downhill, overlooking the marshes, ponds and water-meadows on your left. You are now approaching Thiepval Wood. Take note of the view on your right into a shallow valley, on the south or right side of which is the small and insignificant remnant of Caterpillar Wood. On the south of that wood ran Hamilton Avenue, an important communication trench which ran due east up to the front lines, facing what is today the site of the Memorial to the Missing. North of Caterpillar Wood ran Paisley Avenue, along the south perimeter of the wood, and the trench tramway branch, which served the 32nd Division, next to Paisley Avenue. Both trench and tramway continued alongside the wood and then turned north-east along the eastern face of Thiepval Wood where they ran past Johnstone Post. The south east tip of Thiepval Wood (Q.30.d.5.3) was the main ammunition dump for the infantry of 96 Brigade as they prepared for the opening of the 'Big Push'. Here, as in Authuille Wood, were stored 4,800 Trench Mortar Rounds, 22,000 grenades and 2,000,000 rounds of small arms ammunition. The south western corner of Thiepval Wood was the site of 107 Brigade's headquarters during the opening phase of the battle of the Somme. The Imperial War Graves Commission originally constructed two cemeteries here, Paisley

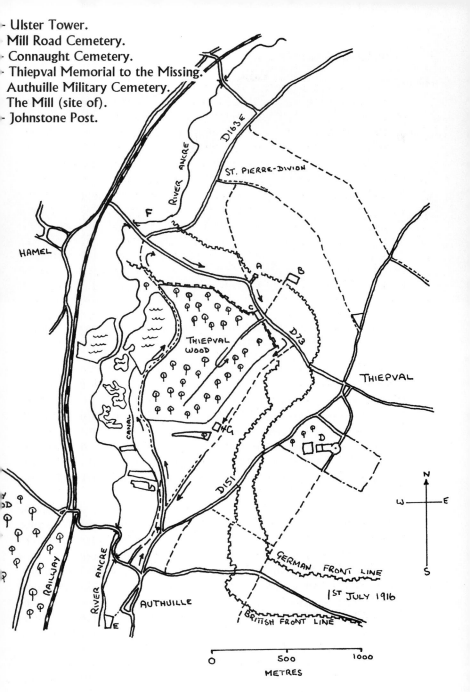

- Ulster Tower.
- Mill Road Cemetery.
- Connaught Cemetery.
- Thiepval Memorial to the Missing.
  Authuille Military Cemetery.
  The Mill (site of).
- Johnstone Post.

Map 23. Thiepval Wood (Bois d'Authuille) area tour.

179

The view towards the Memorial for the Missing from the corner of Thiepval Wood, on the left, past Caterpillar Wood on the right of the valley.

Avenue and Paisley Hillside, which were later removed and concentrated in the Lonsdale Cemetery east of Authuille.

Before proceeding further it is worth looking west across the Ancre towards Mesnil. The valley here was known as the *Passerelle de Magenta*. It was crossed by two vital causeways which were the scene of constant disruption by shellfire and equally constant repair by the R.E. The South Causeway crossed the canalized section of the Ancreat point Q.30..4.1. whilst the North Causeway crossed at Q.3.c.3.6.

Continue your walk keeping to the track on the west of the wood. Running on your immediate left was the tramway branch serving the 36th (Ulster) Division. As this track circuits the western edge of the wood it becomes narrow and rather rough. On your right are the steep slopes where the 15th Royal Irish Rifles, who had been detached from 107 Brigade, were assembled in support of the 11th and 13th Royal Irish Rifles' (108 Brigade) attack past the site of the Ulster Tower, towards Schwaben Redoubt. You will easily find evidence of a major communication trench on your right here. That trench was known as Sutherland Avenue and rose to join Elgin Avenue. Further on these steep slopes also protected many of the Ulster's Field Kitchens which were dug into and operated, until a week before the battle began, at the western end of Ross Street, one of the forest rides which cross the wood. The sites of many of these dugouts and kitchens are still clearly visible today. Ross Street came down the slope opposite the Pumphouse which you will see on your left. Continue along the track until you pass the northern corner of the wood on your right and walk along until you approach the D73, the Mill Road. A position one hundred and eighty yards before the junction of the track with the Mill Road marked the end of organized trenches here, since the valley floor on your left was impossibly muddy and any ditch became waterlogged within minutes. The last outpost was known as Burghead on the right of the track. Peterhead Sap, an important listening post, was situated one hundred and fifty yards to the east on top the embankment which is easily seen across the field.

Turn right onto Mill Road and walk up the slope in an easterly direction. This road neatly bisects the No Man's Land which existed here at the commencement of the Battle of the Somme and indeed through until November's fighting for control of the Ancre Valley north of the Mill Road. On your left you can see the trees surrounding St Pierre Divion which was not attacked on the morning of 1st July. Further up the slope, on your right, a bend in the perimeter of Thiepval Wood marks the junction between 108 and 109 Brigade's attacks on 1st July. That perimeter was guarded by two lines of trenches, many relics of which are still visible today. Soon you will approach a junction where the Thiepval to St. Pierre Divion road leaves the D73. As the Ulstermen crossed No Man's Land this junction also marked the dividing line between 108 and 109 Brigades. In the field to your left are the remnants of a concrete and metal structure which was one of the German front line machine gun posts here. One hundred yards north of the junction lay the German front lines astride which is constructed the Ulster Tower, interestingly at a point known on the British side during 1916 as 'The Pope's Nose'! It fell to the 11th Royal Irish Rifles, the South Antrim Volunteers, to assault this point. No Man's Land was approximately three hundred yards in width along this part of the front.

Follow the Thiepval road, the D73, for a further two hundred yards until you reach Connaught cemetery. This position provides a clear and unobstructed vista. To the north east lies the summit of Schwaben Redoubt and on the spur which leads down from that high ground lies the unique Mill Road cemetery, built on the 'A' lines in front of Schwaben. The cemetery is on such unstable ground that some of the headstones are laid flat to void the unsightly angles and racking which would otherwise be caused by subsidence among the many dugouts and tunnels below. This land was the

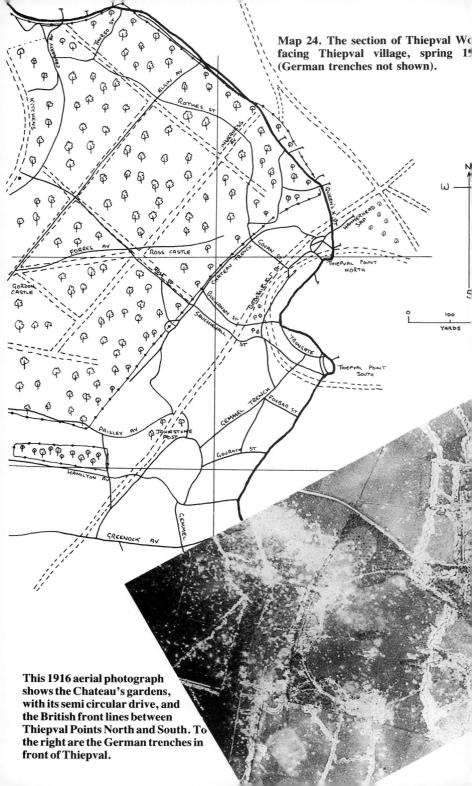

Map 24. The section of Thiepval Wood facing Thiepval village, spring 1916 (German trenches not shown).

This 1916 aerial photograph shows the Chateau's gardens, with its semi circular drive, and the British front lines between Thiepval Points North and South. To the right are the German trenches in front of Thiepval.

scene of 109 Brigade's attack, the right hand boundary of which was the Thiepval communal cemetery, easily seen from Connaught, just north of that village to the left of the water tower.

The interior of Thiepval Wood can be reached along a track which enters the wood by the south-east wall of Connaught cemetery. During 1916 this track, or ride, was known as Inverness Avenue. Parallel and to the north-west ran Elgin Avenue. In his book, *A Brass Hat in No Man's Land*, the then Lieutenant-Colonel Crozier of the 9th Royal Irish Rifles described the awful scenes which the regular shelling of these rides produced. Showing a military colleague around the confines for the first time in early June:

'We wander on and our luck remains out, for, at the junction of Elgin avenue and the fire trench we meet a man with a human arm in his hand. "Whose is that?" I ask. "Rifleman Broderick's, Sir," is the reply. "Where's Broderick?" is my next question. "Up there, Sir," says my informant, pointing to a tree top above our heads. There sure enough is the torn trunk of a man fixed securely in the branches of a shell stripped oak ... out of reach of his comrades.'

Two hundred yards inside the wood Inverness was crossed by another forest ride, known as Whitechurch, where you will find two somewhat dilapidated hunting lodges. Continue along Inverness for a further three hundred yards until you reach the main junction of many rides, in the centre of the wood. This was known as Ross Castle and a number of battalions had their command posts here. The ride to the south east leads directly to the Thiepval Memorial to the Missing, the view which Crozier saw strewn with the bodies of the 32nd Division's men on the morning of 1st July. That to the north-west led to the field kitchens dug in at the slopes above the Ancre. (It is worth noting that you will find great difficulty exiting from the wood on the south and east sides because of barbed wire fences so don't be tempted to take a short cut towards Thiepval if you have walked here to Ross Castle.) A further ride crosses Ross Castle running east to west. This was known as Fores Street and at its western end was a further strong-point known as Gordon Castle where Fores Street joined Elgin Street. By 1st July the wood had been completely stripped of leaves and many of the Ulstermen in the initial assault's support battalions, and 107 Brigade which passed through soon after, were clearly observed from Thiepval fort, suffering terrible casualties within the confines of the wood around Fores Street even before debouching into the open to cross Thiepval Road.

If you chose to walk into Thiepval Wood return to the Connaught cemetery and walk three hundred yards in the direction of Thiepval. This was the frontage of the 9th Royal Inniskilling Fusiliers who were the right hand unit of the initial assault made by the 36th Division. At the foot of the gentle slope you can turn right along the path, marked on the IGN maps, which leads down the valley parallel to the eastern face of Thiepval Wood. In summer this path may be obscured by crop growth but aim for the spire of Authuille church to the left of the trees of Johnstone Post. You are now within the confines of the 32nd Division's battle-front. Two hundred yards down this path it was crossed by Queen's Cross Street, just behind the 1st Salford Pals' front line on 1st July. Hammerhead Sap, where Captain Algeo and his comrades were lost, lay on the south-east side of the path. From here the British front lines travel south past Thiepval in the direction of the Naze and Leipzig Redoubt.

The path running south-westwards and parallel to the wood, known as Broomielaw Street, was the main evacuation trench for casualties on 1st July. For the first five hundred yards of its course the trench ran adjacent to the Chateau's gardens within which the semicircular driveway was a notable feature and where two prominent British salients were located at Thiepval Points North and South. Continue along the south eastern side of the valley keeping the isolated copses of trees on your right. In 1916 this slope gave vital shelter from small arms fire from Thiepval. A little more than one hundred yards from Caterpillar Wood you will pass the remnants of Johnstone Post on your right which could be reached from the west by both the tramway and Paisley Avenue. East of Johnstone Post the British front lines were reached via Causeway Street, thence the support trench known as Gemmel Trench and on into the front lines used by the Tyneside Commercials on 1st July. The area around Johnstone Post is pocked with the collapsed entrances to many dugouts. This is a fine location from which to consider the attacks of the Tyneside Commercials and the Salford Pals, which took place here on 1st July 1916.

From here it is a short walk back along the same track across the fields towards Authuille from where you set out.

Tour Four. Thiepval Village and the German rear defences.

This part of the guide focuses on the autumn fighting for the village and towards the higher ground of Schwaben, Zollern and Staufen redoubts. This can be a relatively short tour, designed to introduce you to the views which can be had from this higher ground. At no point need you be more than eight hundred yards from your car which can be left at the semicircular car parking area adjacent to the memorial. The trench map reference for this spot is R.25.d.5.0. You should be aware that the appearance and layout of the village has changed, in some important respects, from its pre 1914 appearance. If you are feeling energetic the tour can be extended to include the German rear positions along the Grandcourt lines which 107 Brigade's men reached and then lost on the morning of 1st July 1916.

Through the car park, in an east-west direction, ran Joseph Trench. When Thiepval was successfully assaulted by the 18th Division on 26th September Joseph Trench formed the German front line. Of course, by that stage in the summer's fighting all of the Granatloch and Leipzig Redoubt positions had been lost by the German Army. The British troops who made the assault on 26th September formed up two hundred yards south of here, on the south side of the Memorial park, astride the track leading down to the Leipzig salient. During the first twenty four hours of their actions here three Victoria Crosses were won by members of the 18th Division within 600 yards of the memorial car park.

From the car park walk the two hundred yards down the lane leading towards the D151, keeping the memorial gardens on your left. Many of the original German trenches are clearly visible within the memorial park. At the junction you will see the memorial to the 18th Division, which was so ably led here at Thiepval by Ivor Maxse during the autumn fighting of 1916. Looking to your left you can see the orchard below the joint Anglo-French cemetery in the memorial grounds. On July 1st 1916 the German front line crossed the D151 two hundred and twenty yards along that road continuing along a southerly course towards the Leipzig Salient. It was around that point on the Authuille to Thiepval road where the German soldiers stood on their parapets and beckoned the men of the Tyneside Commercials on towards their deaths on that disastrous day. If you look north-west towards the centre of Thiepval Wood the German front line was one hundred and fifty yards away, where Diamond Wood once stood. Although Diamond Wood has long since gone the trees of Oblong

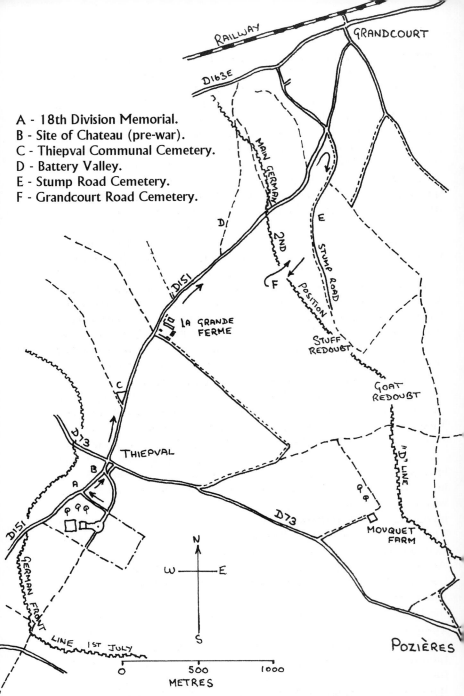

A - 18th Division Memorial.
B - Site of Chateau (pre-war).
C - Thiepval Communal Cemetery.
D - Battery Valley.
E - Stump Road Cemetery.
F - Grandcourt Road Cemetery.

Map 25. Thiepval Village and the area of the German rear defences tour.

Wood, which stood in the middle of No Man's Land beyond Diamond Wood, were still intact until very recently. Oblong Wood stood between Thiepval Points North and South and was connected to the British lines by a sap. It lay in the path of the assault made by the 1st Salford Pals on 1st July 1916. Before the war there was no road between the 18th Division's memorial and the village church because the Chateau's gardens occupied all that ground and ahead as far as Broomielaw Street, hidden in the valley in front of Thiepval Wood (Bois d'Authuille). Martin Middlebrook's magnificent book *The First Day on the Somme* incorrectly described the memorial as standing 'on the site of the ruins of Thiepval Chateau.' This is not so. In order to stand on the site of the original chateau you need to turn right and walk for one hundred and fifty yards, in the direction of the village church, at which point you will be within the courtyard of those original buildings. You will now be opposite the large farm rebuilt on the site which is still owned by the same family who lived here in 1914. This is the scene where two Victoria Crosses were won by two Privates serving with the 12th Middlesex, Private 2442 Frederick Jeremiah Edwards and Private 3281 Robert Ryder, on the afternoon of 26th September during the 18th Division's successful assault on the village.

Walk up to the church. In 1914 this was the village centre. North west of the church a number of farms, houses and outbuildings were located in the quadrant formed by the two roads running north towards the communal cemetery and westwards towards Thiepval Wood. Today, however, all trace of those structures has vanished but this is the scene of the twenty-two year old Second-Lieutenant Tom Edwin Adlam's actions which brought him the Victoria Cross the day after Edwards and Ryder had claimed their place in history. In 1916 the main German communication trench known as *Zollern Graben* (or Lancashire Lane) connecting Thiepval with *Feste Zollern* (Goat Redoubt) ran east-north-eastwards through the gardens of the houses behind the church. Today the reconstructed church is adorned with the village war memorial which is sculpted on one of the buttresses next to the entrance.

Continue past the church, along the D151, in a northerly direction, until you reach the communal cemetery. Before the opening of the Battle of the Somme this cemetery lay 250 yards east of the German front lines. The track, only accessible on foot, which runs past the left or west side of the cemetery is the old Divion Road. Standing here you can look down the Strassburg Lines, an important trench which ran next to the Divion Road and

187

down which the 1/6th Cheshires attacked in the dark before sunrise as part of the 39th Division's assault on St Pierre Divion on the 13th November. On their left the German front line running down to the mill was taken by the 4/5th Black Watch. Five hundred yards to your north-west the Mill Road cemetery can be clearly seen, beyond which stands the Ulster Tower above the slopes which fall away to St Pierre Divion. The Schwaben Redoubt or Parallelogram proper lay above that Divion Road around the site of *la Grande Ferme* which stands six hundred yards further along the D151 past the communal cemetery. The Mill Road Cemetery is therefore not built on the site of that redoubt as many have come to believe, but rather a short distance to the west, between points Cavan, Lisburn and Clones, in the midst of the German 'A' and 'B' lines.

You may now wish to extend this tour and continue along towards the Stump Road area past Schwaben Redoubt. Three hundred yards past the communal cemetery is the 'Crucifix' area, *la Grande Ferme*, which identified the southern tip of the Schwaben Redoubt. The front face of the redoubt ran west-north-west from here and contained at least eleven deep and interconnected shell-proof shelters. This forward face of the Schwaben Redoubt was built 300 metres behind the German front line, but the entire complex of fire trenches which constituted the redoubt overlooked the British positions in Thiepval Wood by a height difference of twenty metres (sixty-five feet). The Schwaben Redoubt was constructed around the 150 metre contour and was located on the west side of the road opposite *la Grande Ferme*. By standing here you can appreciate the extraordinary success achieved by the Ulstermen in gaining this stronghold to quickly on 1st July 191. The Redoubt finally fell during the period 26th September to 5th October 1916 to the 18th Division.

As you move past the site of the Schwaben Redoubt the land begins to fall away on the left of the road. This is 'Battery Valley' which runs down into Grandcourt and which was the site of many hidden German artillery units. On the morning of 1st July 1916 some of the 8th and 9th Royal Irish Rifles had passed across the Schwaben Redoubt and reached the head of this valley before being forced back. This area was the scene of the left flank of the Battle of the Ancre Heights operations undertaken by the 39th Division on 21st October 1916. At the cross roads on the spur just above Grandcourt a narrow lane leads back on your right towards the higher ground east of Schwaben. This is 'Stump Road'. From this lane two British Military cemeteries can be reached. The first of these cemeteries is Stump Road, the second Grandcourt Road Cemetery. Further east, but outside our designated area, is Regina Trench Cemetery, the original part of which was constructed in the winter of 1916-17 but was later enlarged by the concentration of graves from the area between Grandcourt, Miraumont and Courcelette. Stump Road runs out from Grandcourt approximately four hundred metres behind the German second line positions which connected Pozieres to Grandcourt. If you continue to the end of the lane you can look across Stuff and Goat Redoubts (*Feste Staufen* and *Feste Zollern*). Stuff Redoubt marks the furthest point of the Ulster's advance on the morning of 1st July 1916. Stuff Redoubt (trench map reference R.21.c.2.2) is midway between Pozieres and Grandcourt and was not overcome until assaulted by men of the 11th Division during the Battle of Thiepval Ridge between 26-30 September 1916.

pval Wood   Ulster Tower   St Pierre Divion (Below horizon)

The view along the German front line running north of the Thiepval and Mill Roads. This photograph was taken from the communal cemetery just north of Thiepval and looks past both Mill Road Cemetery and the Ulster Tower.

1. This road is not marked on the Official History maps of the conflict and it is therefore easily confused with the road shown on trench maps as running past Johnstone Post and along the east of Thiepval Wood (Bois d'Authuille) to its junction with the D73 Thiepval Road.
2. Charles Douie. *The Weary Road*, Chapter VII entitled Spring in Picardy.
3. Written by Eric Bogle, the song is entitled *No Man's Land* and is sometimes known as the *Green Fields of France*.
4. Public Record Office WO95/2394.

Index.

191

FURTHER READING

My hope is that this guidebook will provide a stepping stone for people who wish to deepen and enhance their knowledge and understanding of the Thiepval Battlefield area. I have tried, throughout the text, to retain sufficient detail for the experienced student but in a style accessible to those of you just starting to develop an interest. In researching this book I have gained most from colleagues and friends. However, the following is a brief list of some of the most easily available written sources used. They have in common the fact that all make reference to locations around the Thiepval area which can be followed through the use if this guide. I have, with one exception, not included the various unit and regimental histories since these are impossibly and increasingly expensive on the second hand market. Such histories, mostly written and published during the 1920s, are, therefore, very difficult to obtain except through reference libraries. Of course the Public Records Office at Kew and the Imperial War Museum in London are the finest sources of primary source material relating to these events.

Edmund Blunden. *Undertones of War* Pub: Richard Cobden-Sanderson, 1928.

Colin Bardgett. *The Lonsdale Battalion* Pub: G.C. Book Publishers Ltd, 1993.

F.P. Crozier. *A Brass Hat in No Man's Land* Pub: Jonathan Cape, 1930.

Charles Douie. *The Weary Road* Pub: 1929, reprinted with additional notes by The Strong Oak Press/Tom Donovan Publishing, 1988.

Cyril Falls. *The History of the 36th (Ulster) Division* Pub: 1922, but reprinted with some additional materials by The Somme Association, 1991.

Tom Johnstone. *Orange, Green & Khaki* Pub: Gill and Macmillan, Dublin, 1992.

Philip Orr. *The Road to the Somme* Pub: The Blackstaff Press, 1987.

Lyn Macdonald. *Somme* Pub: Michael Joseph, 1983.

Martin Middlebrook. *The First Day on the Somme* Pub: Allen Lane, 1971.

Gardiner Mitchell. *Three cheers for the Derrys!* Pub: Yes Publications, Derry, 1991.

Official History of the War, *Military Operations in France and Belgium*, text and map volumes relating to the 1916-18 period. Many volumes now available as reprints from the Imperial War Museum.

Ernest Shephard. *A Sergeant-Major's War* Ed. Bruce Rossor. Pub: The Crowood Press, 1987.

Michael Stedman. *Salford Pals* Pub: Leo Cooper Pen & Sword Books Ltd, 1993.